Language Teaching:
A Scheme for Teacher Education

Editors: C N Candlin and H G Widdowson

Syllabus Design

David Nunan

Oxford University Press

Oxford University Press
Walton Street, Oxford OX2 6DP

Oxford New York Toronto
Delhi Bombay Calcutta Madras Karachi
Petaling Jaya Singapore Hong Kong Tokyo
Nairobi Dar es Salaam Cape Town
Melbourne Auckland

and associated companies in
Berlin Ibadan

OXFORD and OXFORD ENGLISH are
trade marks of Oxford University Press

ISBN 0 19 437139 5

© Oxford University Press 1988
First published 1988
Third impression 1991

Printed in Hong Kong
Typeset by Wyvern Typesetting Ltd, Bristol

Contents

The author and series editors

David Nunan is currently Director of the National Curriculum Resource Centre, which is the teaching, research, and materials development centre for Australia's Adult Migrant Education Program. He has also worked as an ESL/EFL teacher, lecturer, researcher, and consultant in a wide variety of teaching institutions in Australia, Oman, Singapore, Thailand, and the UK. He has published books on language teaching course design, discourse comprehension, learner-centred curriculum development, and the teacher's role as a curriculum developer.

Christopher N. Candlin is Professor of Linguistics in the School of English and Linguistics at Macquarie University, Sydney, having previously been Professor of Applied Linguistics and Director of the Centre for Language in Social Life at the University of Lancaster. He also co-founded and directed the Institute for English Language Education at Lancaster, where he worked on issues in in-service education for teachers.

Henry Widdowson is Professor of English for Speakers of Other Languages at the University of London Institute of Education, having previously been Lecturer in Applied Linguistics at the University of Edinburgh. Before that, he worked on materials development and teacher education as a British Council English Language Officer in Sri Lanka and Bangladesh.

Through work with The British Council, The Council of Europe, and other agencies, both Editors have had extensive and varied experience of language teaching, teacher education, and curriculum development overseas, and both contribute to seminars, conferences, and professional journals.

Introduction

Syllabus Design

The purpose of this book is to provide teachers with tools and techniques for analysing and subjecting to critical scrutiny the syllabuses with which they are working. It is also intended to provide concepts and procedures for those teachers who are in a position to take part in the development of their own syllabuses.

Section One begins with an examination of the concepts of 'syllabus' and 'curriculum'. The rest of the section is concerned with central issues relating to the selection and grading of input in language syllabus design. Concepts and procedures which are examined include needs analysis, goal and objective setting, the selection and grading of content, and the selection and grading of learning tasks.

Section Two closely parallels Section One. Here we shall look at the ways in which the concepts and principles presented in Section One have been applied in practice. Samples of syllabuses and course materials from a range of resources are presented and criticized. The aims of Section Two are as follows:

1 to examine the ways in which the principles set out in Section One have been utilized in syllabus design
2 to provide examples of syllabus design tools, outlines, and planning procedures
3 to provide readers with the opportunity to analyse and assess critically a range of syllabus planning tools, designs, and procedures.

In Section Three, readers are encouraged to apply the ideas developed in Sections One and Two to their own teaching situation. The general aim of the section is to encourage readers to deepen their understanding of the teaching context in which they work. In particular, it is hoped that the tasks will help readers develop a critical attitude towards the syllabus or syllabuses which shape their teaching programmes, and to help them identify ways in which they might modify, adapt, or improve the syllabus or syllabuses with which they work.

Although this book is principally concerned with the selection and grading of input, it is important for syllabus design to be seen as an integral part of the total curriculum. In the course of the book we shall see that syllabus designers are currently facing a dilemma over the relationship between syllabus design and methodology. We shall see that the traditional distinction between syllabus design and methodology becomes difficult to sustain if it is accepted that syllabus design should include the specification of learning tasks and activities.

In attempting to deepen our understanding of language learning and teaching, we may take as our point of departure an analysis of linguistic description at one or more of the levels of pronunciation, vocabulary, grammar, or discourse. Alternatively, we may begin with one or more of the macroskills of listening, speaking, reading, or writing. Finally, we may begin with one or more aspects of teaching, including syllabus design, methodology, task design, content teaching, or evaluation. It is difficult to proceed in any of these areas, however, without taking into consideration the other areas to which it is related. For this reason, this book has been extensively cross-referenced to other volumes in the Scheme. The single most important message in this book is that the effective planning, implementation, and evaluation of language learning and teaching requires an integrated approach in which all the aspects covered in the series are interrelated.

I should like to thank the series editors, Chris Candlin and Henry Widdowson, for the great deal of assistance, guidance, and advice they provided during the writing of this book. Needless to say, the views expressed and the conclusions reached are my own and should not necessarily be attributed to the series editors. Any shortcomings in the book are also mine.

David Nunan

Language Teaching:
A Scheme for Teacher Education

The purpose of this scheme of books is to engage language teachers in a process of continual professional development. We have designed it so as to guide teachers towards the critical appraisal of ideas and the informed application of these ideas in their own classrooms. The scheme provides the means for teachers to take the initiative themselves in pedagogic planning. The emphasis is on critical enquiry as a basis for effective action.

We believe that advances in language teaching stem from the independent efforts of teachers in their own classrooms. This independence is not brought about by imposing fixed ideas and promoting fashionable formulas. It can only occur where teachers, individually or collectively, explore principles and experiment with techniques. Our purpose is to offer guidance on how this might be achieved.

The scheme consists of three sub-series of books covering areas of enquiry and practice of immediate relevance to language teaching and learning. Sub-series 1 focuses on areas of *language knowledge*, with books linked to the conventional levels of linguistic description: pronunciation, vocabulary, grammar, and discourse. Sub-series 2 focuses on different *modes of behaviour* which realize this knowledge. It is concerned with the pedagogic skills of speaking, listening, reading, and writing. Sub-series 3 focuses on a variety of *modes of action* which are needed if this knowledge and behaviour is to be acquired in the operation of language teaching. The books in this sub-series have to do with such topics as syllabus design, the content of language courses, and aspects of methodology, and evaluation.

This sub-division of the field is not meant to suggest that different topics can be dealt with in isolation. On the contrary, the concept of a scheme implies making coherent links between all these different areas of enquiry and activity. We wish to emphasize how their integration formalizes the complex factors present in any teaching process. Each book, then, highlights a particular topic, but also deals contingently with other issues, themselves treated as focal in other books in the series. Clearly, an enquiry into a mode of behaviour like speaking, for example, must also refer to aspects of language knowledge which it realizes. It must also connect to modes of action which can be directed at developing this behaviour in learners. As elements of the whole scheme, therefore, books cross-refer both within and across the different sub-series.

This principle of cross-reference which links the elements of the scheme is also applied to the internal design of the different interrelated books within it. Thus, each book contains three sections, which, by a combination of text and task, engage the reader in a principled enquiry into ideas and practices. The first section of each book makes explicit those theoretical ideas which bear on the topic in question. It provides a conceptual framework for those sections which follow. Here the text has a mainly *explanatory* function, and the tasks serve to clarify and consolidate the points raised. The second section shifts the focus of attention to how the ideas from Section One relate to activities in the classroom. Here the text is concerned with *demonstration*, and the tasks are designed to get readers to evaluate suggestions for teaching in reference both to the ideas from Section One and also to their own teaching experience. In the third section this experience is projected into future work. Here the set of tasks, modelled on those in Section Two, are designed to be carried out by the reader as a combination of teaching techniques and action research in the actual classroom. It is this section that renews the reader's contact with reality: the ideas expounded in Section One and linked to pedagogic practice in Section Two are now to be systematically *tested out* in the process of classroom teaching.

If language teaching is to be a genuinely professional enterprise, it requires continual experimentation and evaluation on the part of practitioners whereby in seeking to be more effective in their pedagogy they provide at the same time — and as a corollary — for their own continuing education. It is our aim in this scheme to promote this dual purpose.

Christopher N. Candlin
Henry Widdowson

Defining syllabus design

1 The scope of syllabus design

1.1 Introduction

We will start by outlining the scope of syllabus design and relating it to the broader field of curriculum development. Later, in **1.4**, we shall also look at the role of the teacher in syllabus design.

Within the literature, there is some confusion over the terms 'syllabus' and 'curriculum'. It would, therefore, be as well to give some indication at the outset of what is meant here by syllabus, and also how syllabus design is related to curriculum development.

▶ TASK 1

As a preliminary activity, write a short definition of the terms 'syllabus' and 'curriculum'.

In language teaching, there has been a comparative neglect of systematic curriculum development. In particular, there have been few attempts to apply, in any systematic fashion, principles of curriculum development to the planning, implementation, and evaluation of language programmes. Language curriculum specialists have tended to focus on only part of the total picture — some specializing in syllabus design, others in methodology, and yet others in assessment and evaluation. In recent years this rather fragmented approach has been criticized, and there have been calls for a more comprehensive approach to language curriculum design (see, for example, Breen and Candlin 1980; Richards 1984; Nunan 1985). The present book is intended to provide teachers with the skills they need to address, in a systematic fashion, the problems and tasks which confront them in their programme planning.

Candlin (1984) suggests that curricula are concerned with making general statements about language learning, learning purpose and experience, evaluation, and the role relationships of teachers and learners. According to Candlin, they will also contain banks of learning items and suggestions about how these might be used in class. Syllabuses, on the other hand, are more localized and are based on accounts and records of what actually happens at the classroom level as teachers and learners apply a given curriculum to their own situation. These accounts can be used to make subsequent modifications to the curriculum, so that the developmental process is ongoing and cyclical.

1.2 A general curriculum model

▶ **TASK 2**

Examine the following planning tasks and decide on the order in which they might be carried out.

— monitoring and assessing student progress
— selecting suitable materials
— stating the objectives of the course
— evaluating the course
— listing grammatical and functional components
— designing learning activities and tasks
— instructing students
— identifying topics, themes, and situations

It is possible to study 'the curriculum' of an educational institution from a number of different perspectives. In the first instance we can look at curriculum planning, that is at decision making, in relation to identifying learners' needs and purposes; establishing goals and objectives; selecting and grading content; organizing appropriate learning arrangements and learner groupings; selecting, adapting, or developing appropriate materials, learning tasks, and assessment and evaluation tools.

Alternatively, we can study the curriculum 'in action' as it were. This second perspective takes us into the classroom itself. Here we can observe the teaching/learning process and study the ways in which the intentions of the curriculum planners, which were developed during the planning phase, are translated into action.

Yet another perspective relates to assessment and evaluation. From this perspective, we would try and find out what students had learned and what they had failed to learn in relation to what had been planned. Additionally, we might want to find out whether they had learned anything which had not been planned. We would also want to account for our findings, to make judgements about why some things had succeeded and others had failed, and perhaps to make recommendations about what changes might be made to improve things in the future.

Finally, we might want to study the management of the teaching institution, looking at the resources available and how these are utilized, how the institution relates to and responds to the wider community, how constraints imposed by limited resources and the decisions of administrators affect what happens in the classroom, and so on.

All of these perspectives taken together represent the field of curriculum study. As we can see, the field is a large and complex one.

It is important that, in the planning, implementation, and evaluation of a given curriculum, all elements be integrated, so that decisions made at one level are not in conflict with those made at another. For instance, in courses based on principles of communicative language teaching, it is important that these principles are reflected, not only in curriculum documents and syllabus plans, but also in classroom activities, patterns of classroom interaction, and in tests of communicative performance.

1.3 Defining 'syllabus'

There are several conflicting views on just what it is that distinguishes syllabus design from curriculum development. There is also some disagreement about the nature of 'the syllabus'. In books and papers on the subject, it is possible to distinguish a broad and a narrow approach to syllabus design.

The narrow view draws a clear distinction between syllabus design and methodology. Syllabus design is seen as being concerned essentially with the selection and grading of content, while methodology is concerned with the selection of learning tasks and activities. Those who adopt a broader view question this strict separation, arguing that with the advent of communicative language teaching the distinction between content and tasks is difficult to sustain.

The following quotes have been taken from Brumfit (1984) which provides an excellent overview of the range and diversity of opinion on syllabus design. The broad and narrow views are both represented in the book, as you will see from the quotes.

▶ TASK 3

As you read the quotes, see whether you can identify which writers are advocating a broad approach and which a narrow approach.

1 . . . I would like to draw attention to a distinction . . . between curriculum or syllabus, that is its content, structure, parts and organisation, and, . . . what in curriculum theory is often called curriculum processes, that is curriculum development, implementation, dissemination and evaluation. The former is concerned with the WHAT of curriculum: what the curriculum is like or should be like; the latter is concerned with the WHO and HOW of establishing the curriculum.
   (*Stern 1984: 10–11*)

2 [The syllabus] replaces the concept of 'method', and the syllabus is now seen as an instrument by which the teacher, with the help of the syllabus designer, can achieve a degree of 'fit' between the needs and aims of the learner (as social being and as individual) and the activities which will take place in the classroom.
   (*Yalden 1984: 14*)

3 ... the syllabus is simply a framework within which activities can
be carried out: a teaching device to facilitate learning. It only
becomes a threat to pedagogy when it is regarded as absolute rules
for determining what is to be learned rather than points of
reference from which bearings can be taken.
(*Widdowson 1984: 26*)

4 We might ... ask whether it is possible to separate so easily what
we have been calling content from what we have been calling
method or procedure, or indeed whether we can avoid bringing
evaluation into the debate?
(*Candlin 1984: 32*)

5 Any syllabus will express—however indirectly—certain assumptions about language, about the psychological process of learning, and about the pedagogic and social processes within a
classroom.
(*Breen 1984: 49*)

6 ... curriculum is a very general concept which involves
consideration of the whole complex of philosophical, social and
administrative factors which contribute to the planning of an
educational program. Syllabus, on the other hand, refers to that
subpart of curriculum which is concerned with a specification of
what units will be taught (as distinct from how they will be
taught, which is a matter for methodology).
(*Allen 1984: 61*)

7 Since language is highly complex and cannot be taught all at the
same time, successful teaching requires that there should be a
selection of material depending on the prior definition of
objectives, proficiency level, and duration of course. This
selection takes place at the syllabus planning stage.
(*op. cit.: 65*)

As you can see, some language specialists believe that syllabus (the selection
and grading of content) and methodology should be kept separate; others
think otherwise. One of the issues you will have to decide on as you work
through this book is whether you think syllabuses should be defined solely
in terms of the selection and grading of content, or whether they should
also attempt to specify and grade learning tasks and activities.

Here, we shall take as our point of departure the rather traditional notion
that a syllabus is a statement of content which is used as the basis for
planning courses of various kinds, and that the task of the syllabus designer
is to select and grade this content. To begin with, then, we shall distinguish
between syllabus design, which is concerned with the 'what' of a language

programme, and methodology, which is concerned with the 'how'. (Later, we shall look at proposals for 'procedural' syllabuses in which the distinction between the 'what' and the 'how' becomes difficult to sustain.)

One document which gives a detailed account of the various syllabus components which need to be considered in developing language courses is *Threshold Level English* (van Ek 1975). van Ek lists the following as necessary components of a language syllabus:

1 the situations in which the foreign language will be used, including the topics which will be dealt with;
2 the language activities in which the learner will engage;
3 the language functions which the learner will fulfil;
4 what the learner will be able to do with respect to each topic;
5 the general notions which the learner will be able to handle;
6 the specific (topic-related) notions which the learner will be able to handle;
7 the language forms which the learner will be able to use;
8 the degree of skill with which the learner will be able to perform.
   (*van Ek 1975: 8–9*)

▶ TASK 4

Do you think that van Ek subscribes to a 'broad' or 'narrow' view of syllabus design?

Which, if any, of the above components do you think are beyond the scope of syllabus design?

1.4 The role of the classroom teacher

In a recent book dealing, among other things, with syllabus design issues, Bell (1983) claims that teachers are, in the main, consumers of other people's syllabuses; in other words, that their role is to implement the plans of applied linguists, government agencies, and so on. While some teachers have a relatively free hand in designing the syllabuses on which their teaching programmes are based, most are likely to be, as Bell suggests, consumers of other people's syllabuses.

▶ TASK 5

Study the following list of planning tasks.

In your experience, for which of these tasks do you see the classroom teacher as having primary responsibility?

Rate each task on a scale from 0 (no responsibility) to 5 (total responsibility).

– identifying learners' communicative needs	0 1 2 3 4 5
– selecting and grading syllabus content	0 1 2 3 4 5
– grouping learners into different classes or learning arrangements	0 1 2 3 4 5
– selecting/creating materials and learning activities	0 1 2 3 4 5
– monitoring and assessing learner progress	0 1 2 3 4 5
– course evaluation	0 1 2 3 4 5

In a recent study of an educational system where classroom teachers are expected to design, implement, and evaluate their own curriculum, one group of teachers, when asked the above question, stated that they saw themselves as having primary responsibility for all of the above tasks except for the third one (grouping learners). Some of the teachers in the system felt quite comfortable with an expanded professional role. Others felt that syllabus development should be carried out by people with specific expertise, and believed that they were being asked to undertake tasks for which they were not adequately trained (Nunan 1987).

► TASK 6

What might be the advantages and/or disadvantages of teachers in your system designing their own syllabuses?

Can you think of any reasons why teachers might be discouraged from designing, or might not want to design their own syllabuses?

Are these reasons principally pedagogic, political, or administrative?

1.5 Conclusion

In 1, I have tried to provide some idea of the scope of syllabus design. I have suggested that traditionally syllabus design has been seen as a subsidiary component of curriculum design. 'Curriculum' is concerned with the planning, implementation, evaluation, management, and administration of education programmes. 'Syllabus', on the other hand, focuses more narrowly on the selection and grading of content.

While it is realized that few teachers are in the position of being able to design their own syllabuses, it is hoped that most are in a position to interpret and modify their syllabuses in the process of translating them into action. The purpose of this book is therefore to present the central issues and options available for syllabus design in order to provide teachers with the necessary knowledge and skills for evaluating, and, where feasible, modifying and adapting the syllabuses with which they work. At the very least, this book should help you understand (and therefore more effectively exploit) the syllabuses and course materials on which your programmes are based.

► ## TASK 7

Look back at the definitions you wrote in Task 1 and rewrite these in the light of the information presented in **1**.

In what ways, if any, do your revised definitions differ from the ones you wrote at the beginning?

In **2**, we shall look at some of the starting points in syllabus design. The next central question to be addressed is, 'Where does syllabus content come from?' In seeking answers to this question, we shall look at techniques for obtaining information from and about learners for use in syllabus design. We shall examine the controversy which exists over the very nature of language itself and how this influences the making of decisions about what to include in the syllabus. We shall also look at the distinction between product-oriented and process-oriented approaches to syllabus design. These two orientations are studied in detail in **3** and **4**. The final part of Section One draws on the content of the preceding parts and relates this content to the issue of objectives. You will be asked to consider whether or not we need objectives, and if so, how these should be formulated.

2 Points of departure

2.1 Introduction

In 1 it was argued that syllabus design was essentially concerned with the selection and grading of content. As such, it formed a sub-component of the planning phase of curriculum development. (You will recall that the curriculum has at least three phases: a planning phase, an implementation phase, and an evaluation phase.)

The first question to confront the syllabus designer is where the content is to come from in the first place. We shall now look at the options available to syllabus designers in their search for starting points in syllabus design.

▶ ## TASK 8

Can you think of any ways in which our beliefs about the nature of language and learning might influence our decision-making on what to put into the syllabus and how to grade it?

If we had consensus on just what it was that we were supposed to teach in order for learners to develop proficiency in a second or foreign language; if we knew a great deal more than we do about language learning; if it were possible to teach the totality of a given language, and if we had complete descriptions of the target language, problems associated with selecting and sequencing content and learning experiences would be relatively straight-forward. As it happens, there is not a great deal of agreement within the teaching profession on the nature of language and language learning. As a consequence, we must make judgements in selecting syllabus components from all the options which are available to us. As Breen (1984) points out, these judgements are not value-free, but reflect our beliefs about the nature of language and learning. In this and the other parts in this section, we shall see how value judgements affect decision-making in syllabus design.

The need to make value judgements and choices in deciding what to include in (or omit from) specifications of content and which elements are to be the basic building blocks of the syllabus, presents syllabus designers with constant problems. The issue of content selection becomes particularly pressing if the syllabus is intended to underpin short courses. (It could be argued that the shorter the course, the greater the need for precision in content specification.)

2.2 Basic orientations

Until fairly recently, most syllabus designers started out by drawing up lists of grammatical, phonological, and vocabulary items which were then graded according to difficulty and usefulness. The task for the learner was seen as gaining mastery over these grammatical, phonological, and vocabulary items.

> Learning a language, it was assumed, entails mastering the elements or building blocks of the language and learning the rules by which these elements are combined, from phoneme to morpheme to word to phrase to sentence.
> (*Richards and Rodgers 1986: 49*)

During the 1970s, communicative views of language teaching began to be incorporated into syllabus design. The central question for proponents of this new view was, 'What does the learner want/need to do with the target language?' rather than, 'What are the linguistic elements which the learner needs to master?' Syllabuses began to appear in which content was specified, not only in terms of the grammatical elements which the learners were expected to master, but also in terms of the functional skills they would need to master in order to communicate successfully.

This movement led in part to the development of English for Specific Purposes (ESP). Here, syllabus designers focused, not only on language functions, but also on experiential content (that is, the subject matter through which the language is taught).

Traditionally, linguistically-oriented syllabuses, along with many so-called communicative syllabuses, shared one thing in common: they tended to focus on the things that learners should know or be able to do as a result of instruction. In the rest of this book we shall refer to syllabuses in which content is stated in terms of the outcomes of instruction as 'product-oriented'.

As we have already seen, a distinction is traditionally drawn between syllabus design, which is concerned with outcomes, and methodology, which is concerned with the process through which these outcomes are to be brought about. Recently, however, some syllabus designers have suggested that syllabus content might be specified in terms of learning tasks and activities. They justify this suggestion on the grounds that communication is a process rather than a set of products.

In evaluating syllabus proposals, we have to decide whether this view represents a fundamental change in perspective, or whether those advocating process syllabuses have made a category error; whether, in fact, they are really addressing methodological rather than syllabus issues. This is something which you will have to decide for yourself as you work through this book.

▶ ## TASK 9

At this stage, what is your view on the legitimacy of defining syllabuses in terms of learning processes? Do you think that syllabuses should list and grade learning tasks and activities as well as linguistic content?

A given syllabus will specify all or some of the following: grammatical structures, functions, notions, topics, themes, situations, activities, and tasks. Each of these elements is either product or process oriented, and the inclusion of each will be justified according to beliefs about the nature of language, the needs of the learner, or the nature of learning.

In the rest of this book, we shall be making constant references to and comparisons between *process* and *product*. What we mean when we refer to 'process' is a series of actions directed toward some end. The 'product' is the end itself. This may be clearer if we consider some examples. A list of grammatical structures is a product. Classroom drilling undertaken by learners in order to learn the structures is a process. The interaction of two speakers as they communicate with each other is a process. A tape recording of their conversation is a product.

▶ ## TASK 10

Complete the following table, to indicate whether each of the syllabus elements is product or process oriented. Under the heading 'reference', indicate whether this particular element would be selected by the syllabus designer with reference to the learner, the target language, or to some theory of learning. (The first one has been done for you.)

Element	Orientation	Reference
Structures	*Product*	*Language*
Functions		
Notions		
Topics		
Themes		
Subjects		
Activities		
Tasks		

Table 1

Did you find that some elements could be assigned to more than one orientation or point of reference? Which were these?

2.3 Learning purpose

In recent years, a major trend in language syllabus design has been the use of information from and about learners in curriculum decision-making. In this section, we shall look at some of the ways in which learner data have been used to inform decision-making in syllabus design. In the course of the discussion we shall look at the controversy over general and specific purpose syllabus design.

Assumptions about the learner's purpose in undertaking a language course, as well as the syllabus designer's beliefs about the nature of language and learning can have a marked influence on the shape of the syllabus on which the course is based. Learners' purposes will vary according to how specific they are, and how immediately learners wish to employ their developing language skills.

▶ ## TASK 11

Which of the following statements represent specific language needs and which are more general?

'I want to be able to talk to my neighbours in English.'
'I want to study microbiology in an English-speaking university.'
'I want to develop an appreciation of German culture by studying the language.'
'I want to be able to communicate in Greek.'
'I want my daughter to study French at school so she can matriculate and read French at university.'
'I want to read newspapers in Indonesian.'
'I want to understand Thai radio broadcasts.'
'I need "survival" English.'
'I want to be able to read and appreciate French literature.'
'I want to get a better job at the factory.'
'I want to speak English.'
'I want to learn English for nursing.'

For which of the above would it be relatively easy to predict the grammar and topics to be listed in the syllabus?

For which would it be difficult to predict the grammar and topics?

Techniques and procedures for collecting information to be used in syllabus design are referred to as needs analysis. These techniques have been borrowed and adapted from other areas of training and development, particularly those associated with industry and technology.

▶ TASK 12

One general weakness of most of the literature on needs analysis is the tendency to think only in terms of learner needs. Can you think of any other groups whose needs should be considered?

Information will need to be collected, not only on why learners want to learn the target language, but also about such things as societal expectations and constraints and the resources available for implementing the syllabus.

Broadly speaking, there are two different types of needs analysis used by language syllabus designers. The first of these is learner analysis, while the second is task analysis.

Learner analysis is based on information about the learner. The central question of concern to the syllabus designer is: 'For what purpose or purposes is the learner learning the language?' There are many other subsidiary questions, indeed it is possible to collect a wide range of information as can be seen from the following data collection forms.

Appendix A

Sample needs analysis survey form.

This form was developed for use at the Pennington Migrant Education Centre, South Australia. Students complete the form with assistance from bilingual information officers.

Date:_____ASLPR_____

                                                        L S R W

Name:_____Address:_____

Age:_____Country of Origin:_____

Family: M.S.W.D. No. of Children:_____Ages:_____

Other relatives in Australia:_____

Elsewhere:_____

Education: No. of years:_____Qualifications:_____
              Why study finished:_____
              English study:_____

Employment: Main occupation:_____
              Other jobs held:_____
              In Australia:_____
              Type of work sought:_____

Interests: e.g. hobbies, sports, leisure activities:_____
              Skills:_____

First language: _____Others spoken:_____
                                      Others studied:_____

Language learning:
A. Do you like to learn English by READING
                                    WRITING
                                    LISTENING AND SPEAK-
                                    ING
                                    OTHER
   which do you like the most?_____
B. Do you like to study grammar
                 learn new words
                 practise the sounds and pronunciation?
   Which do you like the most?_____
C. Do you like to learn English by:
              _____   cassettes
              _____   games
              _____   talking to English speakers
              _____   studying English books
              _____   watching T.V.
Which is the most important (1—5) to you?_____
D. Macroskills
   1. Reading:
      (a) Can you use a dictionary
          —a little _____ very well _____
      (b) What can you read in English:
                          simple stories
                          newspapers
                          forms: bank
                                 P.O.
                                 C.E.S.
                          advertisements: shopping
                                          housing
                                          employment
                          bus timetables
                          maps/directories
                          school notes
      (c) What are the most important for you to learn
          now:_____
      2. Writing:
         (d) Do you ever write letters
                          notes to teachers
                          fill in forms
         (e) Which is the most important for you to learn
             now:_____
      3. Listening and speaking:

                                        _____
         (f) Who do you speak
             with in English?   (g) How much do you
                                        understand?

                                        _____
                                        0 a little a lot 100%

Shop assistants
Neighbours and friends
Bus drivers
Medical people
Teachers
Employers
Others

(h) Who is it most important for you to learn to speak with now?_____
(i) Do you watch T.V.
    listen to the radio
(j) How much do you understand?

E. How do you learn best?

	No	A little	Good	Best
alone				
pairs				
small group				
class				
outside class				

F. What do you feel are the most important things for you to learn in the: short term_____
                                                                              long term_____

G. How much time is available for study now:
                                                 per day_____
                                                 per week_____
   Where would you like to study:
                                                 I.L.C._____
                                                 Home_____

H. Agreement:
   Length ___/___/___ to ___/___/___
   How often do you want supervision:
I. Date of first supervision ___/___/___
   Comments (may include impressions of interviewer/interpreter):
J. Interviewer:_____
   Interpreter:_____
   Date:_____

(*Nunan 1985: 67–70*)

Interviewer:	Date:

Name:

Current proficiency level:

Age:

Years of formal education:

Number and type of previous courses:

Nationality:

Marital status:

Length of time in target country:

Present occupation:

Intended occupation:

Home language:

Other languages spoken:

Preferences relating to methodology:

course length:

intensity:

Learning style:

Purpose in coming to class:

Language goals:

Life goals:

(*Nunan and Burton 1985*)

▶ TASK 13

Which of the above information do you think is likely to be most useful for planning purposes?

What are some of the purposes to which the information might be put?

The information can serve many purposes, depending on the nature of the educational institution in which it is to be used. In the first instance, it can guide the selection of content. It may also be used to assign learners to class groupings. This will be quite a straightforward matter if classes are based solely on proficiency levels, but much more complicated if they are designed to reflect the goals and aspirations of the learners. In addition, the data can be used by the teacher to modify the syllabus and methodology so they are more acceptable to the learners, or to alert the teacher to areas of possible conflict.

▶ **TASK 14**

What sort of problems might the teacher be alerted to?

How, in your opinion, might these be dealt with?

With certain students, for example older learners or those who have only experienced traditional educational systems, there are numerous areas of possible conflict within a teaching programme. These potential points of conflict can be revealed through needs analysis. For example, the data might indicate that the majority of learners desire a grammatically-based syllabus with explicit instruction. If teachers are planning to follow a non-traditional approach, they may need to negotiate with the learners and modify the syllabus to take account of learner perceptions about the nature of language and language learning. On the other hand, if they are strongly committed to the syllabus with which they are working, or if the institution is fairly rigid, they may wish to concentrate, in the early part of the course, on activities designed to convince learners of the value of the approach being taken.

▶ **TASK 15**

Some syllabus designers differentiate between 'objective' and 'subjective' information.

What do you think each of these terms refers to?

Which of the items in the sample data collection forms in Task 12 relate to 'objective' information, and which to 'subjective' information?

'Objective' data is that factual information which does not require the attitudes and views of the learners to be taken into account. Thus, biographical information on age, nationality, home language, etc. is said to be 'objective'. 'Subjective' information, on the other hand, reflects the perceptions, goals, and priorities of the learner. It will include, among other things, information on why the learner has undertaken to learn a second language, and the classroom tasks and activities which the learner prefers.

The second type of analysis, task analysis, is employed to specify and categorize the language skills required to carry out real-world communicative tasks, and often follows the learner analysis which establishes the communicative purposes for which the learner wishes to learn the language. The central question here is: 'What are the subordinate skills and knowledge required by the learner in order to carry out real-world communicative tasks?'

▶ **TASK 16**

Dick and Carey (1978) describe a number of instructional analysis approaches, including procedural analysis, which is used when an ordered sequence of behaviours is required to achieve a particular task. The tasks below must be carried out to make a long-distance phone call. In what order do you think these tasks need to be carried out for a long distance call to be made successfully?

– Dial the appropriate area code.
– Ask for the desired person.
– Lift the receiver and listen for the appropriate dial tone.
– Locate the telephone number of the desired person
  and write it down.
– Listen for call signal.
– Locate the area code and write it down.
– Dial the telephone number noted.

What sorts of communication tasks might be amenable to such an analysis?

One of the things which many second language learners want to do is comprehend radio and television broadcasts. Using the above list as a guide, write down the various skills and knowledge which would be required for a learner to understand a radio weather report.

The most sophisticated application of needs analysis to language syllabus design is to be found in the work of John Munby (1978). The model developed by Munby contains nine elements. According to Munby, it is important for the syllabus designer to collect information on each of these components:

1 Participant
Under this component is specified information relating to the learner's identity and language skills. These will include age, sex, nationality, mother tongue, command of target language, other languages, etc. It is therefore similar in some respects to the learner analysis which has already been described.

2 Purposive domain
This category refers to the purposes for which the target language is required.

3 Setting
Under this parameter, the syllabus designer must consider the environments in which the target language will be employed.

4 Interaction

Here, the syllabus designer needs to consider the people with whom the learner will be interacting. (See the discussion on role sets in Wright: *Roles of Teachers and Learners* published in this Scheme.)

5 Instrumentality

Instrumentality refers to the medium (whether the language is spoken or written, receptive or productive), the mode (whether the communication is monologue or dialogue, written or spoken, to be heard or read), and the channel (whether the communication is face-to-face or indirect). (See Bygate: *Speaking* published in this Scheme.)

6 Dialect

Here the variety and/or dialect is specified.

7 Target level

Here is stated the degree of mastery which the learner will need to gain over the target language.

8 Communicative event

This refers to the productive and receptive skills the learner will need to master.

9 Communicative key

Here, the syllabus designer needs to specify the interpersonal attitudes and tones the learner will be required to master.

▶ TASK 17

Do you think that the Munby approach is principally concerned with the collection of objective or subjective information?

The Munby approach has received criticism from many quarters for being too mechanistic, and for paying too little attention to the perceptions of the learner. As it is also developed with reference to individual learners, it may ultimately be self-defeating for classroom teaching.

Criticisms of early needs analysis work led to a change of emphasis, with a greater focus on the collection and utilization of 'subjective' information in syllabus design. This change in emphasis reflected a trend towards a more humanistic approach to education in general. Humanistic education is based on the belief that learners should have a say in *what* they should be learning and *how* they should learn it, and reflects the notion that education should be concerned with the development of autonomy in the learner. Apart from philosophical reasons for weaning learners from dependence on teachers and educational systems, it is felt, particularly in systems where there are insufficient resources to provide a complete education, that learners should be taught independent learning skills so they may continue their education after the completion of formal instruction.

Like most other aspects of language syllabus design, needs analysis procedures have attracted criticism from a variety of sources—from teachers who feel learner independence detracts from their own authority and status in the classroom, from some education authorities who feel that syllabus decisions should be made by experts not learners, and by some learners themselves who feel that, if a teacher or institution asks for the learner's opinion, it is a sign that they do not know what they are doing.

The discussion relating to the role of the learner in syllabus design illustrates the point made in 1, that most decisions are underpinned by value judgements derived from the planner's belief systems. All syllabuses, indeed, all aspects of the curriculum, including methodology and learner assessment and evaluation are underpinned by beliefs about the nature of language and language learning.

▶ **TASK 18**

> What views on the nature of language and language learning do you think underly the Munby view of needs-based syllabus design as this has been described above?

The approach to syllabus design promoted by Munby has led, in some instances, to syllabuses with a narrow focus such as 'English for Motor Mechanics' and 'English for Biological Science'. The assumption behind the development of some such syllabuses is that there are certain aspects of language which are peculiar to the contexts in which it is used and the purposes for which it is used. For example, it is assumed that there are certain structures, functions, topics, vocabulary items, conceptual meanings, and so on that are peculiar to the world of the motor mechanic and which are not found in 'general' English.

It is also assumed that different areas of use will require different communication skills from the learner, and that these need to be specifically taught for the area of use in question.

▶ **TASK 19**

> Do you have any reservations about these views?

For most people, the idea that a given language is divided into lots of subordinate and discrete 'universes of discourse' or 'mini-languages' is unsatisfactory. It does not seem to be consistent with their own experience of language. Analysis of the language used in different domains seems to indicate that, apart from certain technical terms, linguistic elements are remarkably similar. It is argued that, whatever learners' final communicative purposes are, they should be taught those elements that represent a 'common core' of language.

It has also been pointed out that the great majority of learners want 'general English' rather than English for the sorts of specific purposes indicated above. However, there is controversy over just what it is which constitutes 'general English'.

▶ # TASK 20

Study the following quote:

> If we say that X speaks Chinese . . . we do not mean that X can only give a lecture on engineering in Chinese . . . Rather, when we say that someone can speak a language, we mean that that person can speak the language in the sorts of situations people commonly encounter. That is, there are certain everyday situations in which we, as human beings living in a physical and social world, are necessarily involved. We must all, for example, obtain food and shelter, we must find our way about, and we must establish relationships with other people. General proficiency, then, refers to the ability to use language in these everyday, non-specialist situations.
> (*Ingram 1984: 10*)

How convincing do you find this description of 'general' language proficiency?

The difficulty here is in deciding just what constitutes the common, everyday purposes of English. It is conceivable that this 'general' component may, in itself, represent simply another domain of use for the second language learner. In fact, researchers have demonstrated that, for both first and second language learners, the contexts in which they are called upon to use language can have a marked effect on their ability to communicate effectively in that situation. For example, certain individuals, who are quite competent at 'social' or 'survival' English, as described by Ingram, are seriously disadvantaged when they have to use English at school. In fact, even children who are native speakers sometimes have difficulty when they begin formal schooling. It has been suggested that this is due to the unfamiliar uses to which language is being put. In other words, difficulty is not so much at the level of grammar and vocabulary but at the level of discourse. (See Widdowson (1983) for an extended discussion on this aspect of language.)

The debate over the nature of language has not been helped by a confusion between the nature of the language used in particular communicative contexts, the skills involved in communicating in these contexts, and the means whereby these skills might be acquired. Consider, as an example, the student who wants to learn English in order to study motor mechanics. It might well be that, apart from a few specialist terms, the structures, functions, and general notions used by an instructor in describing the construction and functions of a carburettor are basically derived from the same common stock as those used by someone having a casual conversation with their neighbour. However, this does not mean that someone who has developed skills in conducting a casual conversation will necessarily be able to follow the unfamiliar discourse patterns and rhetorical routines underlying, say, a lecture on the structure and function of the carburettor. In addition, it does not necessarily follow that the best way to develop the listening skills required to study motor mechanics is to listen to repeated mini-lectures on the nature of carburettors and other such topics. It may well follow, but this is not self-evident.

▶ ## TASK 21

In answering the following questions, try and justify your position by stating why you think the tasks are or are not equivalent in terms of the skills the learner will need to carry out the tasks.

1 If someone were able to give a lecture on engineering in Chinese, do you think they would also be able to describe symptoms of illness to a doctor?
2 If someone were able to describe symptoms of illness to a doctor in Chinese, do you think they would also be able to give a lecture on engineering?
3 Would someone who is able to describe symptoms of illness to a doctor in English also be able to work as a waiter in an English-speaking restaurant?
4 Would someone who is capable of working as a waiter in an English-speaking restaurant also be able to describe symptoms of illness to a doctor?

Many teachers would agree with Ingram that there is such a thing as 'general English ability' and that this can be defined as the ability to carry out commonly occurring real-world tasks. If asked to make a list of these tasks, they would probably list such things as asking for directions, asking for and providing personal details, describing symptoms of illness to a doctor, understanding the radio, reading newspapers, writing notes to a teacher, and so on. In fact they could probably generate endless lists of 'common everyday tasks'. Now, common sense would suggest that it is not necessary for each and every task to be taught in the classroom. In fact, it would be an impossibility. What the syllabus designer and the teacher must decide is which classroom tasks will ensure maximum transfer of learning to tasks which have not been taught. On the one hand, we can make a random selection of real-world tasks and teach these in the hope that the relevant bits of language 'stick' as it were, and that transfer to other tasks will occur. On the other hand, we can select tasks which may bear little resemblance to real-world tasks but which are assumed to stimulate internal psychological learning processes. The traditional classroom substitution drill would be an example of a classroom task which is justified, not because the learner might want to engage in drills outside the classroom, but because it is assumed to result in learning which can be transferred to real-world communicative language use. (We shall return to this important issue later in the section.)

Widdowson has written extensively on the distinction between general purpose English (GPE) and English for specific purposes. He suggests that ESP has a training function which is aimed at the development of 'restricted competence', whereas GPE fulfils an educative function and is aimed at the development of 'general capacity'.

> . . . ESP is essentially a training operation which seeks to provide learners with a restricted competence to enable them to cope with certain clearly defined tasks. These tasks constitute the specific purposes which the ESP course is designed to meet. The course, therefore, makes direct reference to eventual aims. GPE, on the other hand, is essentially an educational operation which seeks to provide learners with a general capacity to enable them to cope with undefined eventualities in the future. Here, since there are no definite aims which can determine course content, there has to be recourse to intervening objectives formulated by pedagogic theory. . . . in GPE, the actual use of language occasioned by communicative necessity is commonly a vague and distant prospect on the other side of formal assessment.
> (*Widdowson 1983: 6*)

► ## TASK 22

How convincing do you find this line of argument?

Do you think it necessarily follows that teaching for a specific purpose will lead to a restricted competence?

2.4 Learning goals

An important step in the development of a language programme is identifying learning goals. These will provide a rationale for the course or programme. Learning goals may be derived from a number of sources, including task analysis, learner data, ministry of education specifications, and so on. The nature of the courses to be derived from syllabus specifications, the length of the courses, and many other factors will determine what is feasible and appropriate to set as goals, and will also largely dictate the types of communicative and pedagogic objectives which are both appropriate and feasible for the educational system in question.

▶ TASK 23

Study the following goal statements:

'To encourage learners to develop confidence in using the target language.'
'To develop skills in monitoring performance in spoken language.'
'To establish and maintain relationships through exchanging information, ideas, opinions, attitudes, feelings, experiences, and plans.'
'To develop the ability to study, in English, at university.'

In what ways are these statements similar? In what ways are they different?

Based on these statements, how would you define the term 'goal'?

Although they could all be applied to language courses of various sorts, the above statements differ in their focus. They include an affective goal, a learning goal, a communicative goal, and a cognitive goal.

As it is used here, the term 'goal' refers to the general purposes for which a language programme is being taught or learned. While we shall take into consideration a variety of goal types, the focus will be principally on communicative goals. These are defined as the general communicative activities in which the learners will engage (or, in the case of foreign language learning, could potentially engage) in real-world target language use.

If some form of needs analysis has been carried out to establish the purposes and needs of a given group of learners or of an educational system, a necessary second step is to translate them into instructional goals. This requires judgement, particularly to ensure that the goals are appropriate, not only to learner needs, but also to the constraints of the educational institution or system, and the length and scope of programme based on the syllabus. Thus, a syllabus designed for 900 hours of secondary school instruction will be able to incorporate more goals than a 150-hour course for immigrants or refugees. By examining the goal statements of a language programme, one can usually identify the value judgements and belief systems from which they are derived. It is also usually possible to identify whether the syllabus designer has taken as his or her point of departure the language, the learner, or the learning process.

2.5 Conclusion

In looking at starting points in syllabus design, I have suggested that the starting point can be an analysis of the language, information about the learner, beliefs about the learning process itself, or a combination of these.

The key question in relation to a linguistic perspective is: 'What linguistic elements should be taught?' From a learner perspective, the key question is: 'What does the learner want to do with the language?' Finally, from a learning perspective, the key question is: 'What activities will stimulate or promote language acquisition?'

These perspectives are not mutually exclusive. Rather, they represent areas of relative emphasis, and a syllabus designer will usually incorporate insights from all three perspectives.

It has been suggested that there is a major conceptual distinction between product-oriented and process-oriented syllabuses, and that a given syllabus can be located somewhere along a process/product continuum. In 3 and 4 we shall consider product-oriented and process-oriented syllabuses in detail.

3 Product-oriented syllabuses

3.1 Introduction

In **2**, I drew a distinction between product-oriented and process-oriented syllabuses. We saw that product syllabuses are those in which the focus is on the knowledge and skills which learners should gain as a result of instruction, while process syllabuses are those which focus on the learning experiences themselves.

In **3**, we shall look at syllabus proposals which are specified in terms of the end products of a course of instruction. As we shall see, these may be realized in a variety of ways, for example as lists of grammatical items, vocabulary items, language functions, or experiential content.

3.2 Analytic and synthetic syllabus planning

There are many different ways in which syllabus proposals of one sort or another might be analysed. One dimension of analysis which has been the subject of a great deal of discussion and comment is the synthetic/analytic dimension.

It was Wilkins (1976) who first drew attention to the distinction between synthetic and analytic syllabuses. He described the synthetic approach in the following terms:

> A synthetic language teaching strategy is one in which the different parts of language are taught separately and step by step so that acquisition is a process of gradual accumulation of parts until the whole structure of language has been built up.
> (*Wilkins 1976: 2*)

► TASK 24

In his work, Wilkins assumes that grammatical criteria will be used to break the global language down into discrete units. The items will be graded according to the grammatical complexity of the items, their frequency of occurrence, their contrastive difficulty in relation to the learner's first language, situational need, and pedagogic convenience.

Do you think that grammar is the only criterion for selecting and grading content in a synthetic syllabus?

If not, what other criteria can you suggest for selecting and grading content?

Initially, people tended to equate synthetic approaches with grammatical syllabuses. However some applied linguists feel that the term 'synthetic' need not necessarily be restricted to grammatical syllabuses, but may be applied to any syllabus in which the content is product-oriented; that is, which is specified as discrete lists of grammatical items and in which the classroom focus is on the teaching of these items as separate and discrete (see, for example, Widdowson 1979). (Note that in this book, the terms 'grammatical' and 'structural' are used interchangeably.)

In contrast with synthetic syllabuses, analytic syllabuses:

> are organised in terms of the purposes for which people are learning language and the kinds of language performance that are necessary to meet those purposes.
> (*Wilkins 1975: 13*)

In an analytic syllabus, learners are presented with chunks of language which may include structures of varying degrees of difficulty. The starting point for syllabus design is not the grammatical system of the language, but the communicative purposes for which language is used.

It is theoretically possible to conceive of language courses as being solely synthetic or solely analytic. However, it is likely that, in practice, courses will be typified as more-or-less synthetic or more-or-less analytic according to the prominence given to discrete elements in the selection and grading of input.

3.3 Grammatical syllabuses

The most common syllabus type was, and probably still is, one in which syllabus input is selected and graded according to grammatical notions of simplicity and complexity. Later in 3 we shall see that grammatical complexity does not necessarily equate with learning difficulty. In other words, what is grammatically complex will not necessarily be that which is difficult to learn, and that which is grammatically simple will not necessarily be that which is easy to learn.

The most rigid grammatical syllabuses supposedly introduced one item at a time and required mastery of that item before moving on to the next. According to McDonough:

> The transition from lesson to lesson is intended to enable material in one lesson to prepare the ground for the next; and conversely for material in the next to appear to grow out of the previous one.
> (*McDonough 1981: 21*)

McDonough illustrates this point as follows:

Lesson (l)	has drilled copula and adjective combinations: *She is happy*
Lesson (m)	introduces the *-ing* form: *She is driving a car*
Lesson (n)	reintroduces existential *there*: *There is a man standing near the car*
Lesson (o)	distinguishes between mass and count nouns: *There are some oranges and some cheese on the table*
Lesson (p)	introduces the verbs *like* and *want*: *I like oranges but not cheese*
Lesson (q)	reintroduces *don't* previously known in negative imperatives: *I don't like cheese*
Lesson (r)	introduces verbs with stative meaning: *I don't come from Newcastle*
Lesson (s)	introduces adverbs of habit and thus the present simple tense; or rather, present tense in simple aspect: *I usually come at six o'clock*

(*McDonough 1981: 21*)

► TASK 25

As we have already noted, all syllabus outlines or proposals are underpinned by assumptions about the nature of language and language learning.

What assumptions about language and language learning do you imagine might underpin a grammatical syllabus of the type described above?

The assumption behind most grammatical syllabuses seems to be that language consists of a finite set of rules which can be combined in various ways to make meaning. It is further assumed that these rules can be learned one by one, in an additive fashion, each item being mastered on its own before being incorporated into the learner's pre-existing stock of knowledge. The principal purpose of language teaching is to help learners to 'crack the code'. Rutherford (1987) calls this the 'accumulated entities' view of language learning.

Assumptions are also made about language transfer. It is generally assumed that once learners have internalized the formal aspects of a given piece of language, they will automatically be able to use it in genuine communication outside the classroom.

One of the difficulties in designing grammatical 'chains' in which discrete grammatical items are linked is that the links can be rather tenuous. It is also difficult to isolate and present one discrete item at a time, particularly if one wants to provide some sort of context for the language. In addition, evidence from second language acquisition (SLA) research suggests that learning does not occur in this simple additive fashion.

The dilemma for the syllabus designer who is attempting to follow some sort of structural progression in sequencing input is this: How does one control input and yet at the same time provide language samples for the learner to work on which bear some semblance at least to the sort of language the learner will encounter outside the classroom?

This problem might be addressed in a number of ways. One solution would be to abandon any attempt at structural grading. Another might be to use the list of graded structures, not to determine the language to which learners are exposed, but to determine the items which will be the pedagogic focus in class. In other words, learners would be exposed to naturalistic samples of text which were only roughly graded, and which provided a richer context, but they would only be expected formally to master those items which had been isolated, graded, and set out in the syllabus. Another alternative, and one we shall look at in detail in 4, is to focus on what learners are expected to *do* with the language (i.e. learning tasks), rather than on the language itself. With this alternative, it is the tasks rather than the language which are graded.

▶ TASK 26

At this stage, you might like to consider the different suggestions above and rank them from most to least satisfactory.

Can you think of any other ways of addressing the problem of controlling input while at the same time using 'naturalistic' language?

3.4 Criticizing grammatical syllabuses

During the 1970s, the use of structural syllabuses came under increasing criticism. In this section we shall look at some of these criticisms.

One early criticism was that structurally-graded syllabuses misrepresented the nature of that complex phenomenon, language. They did so in tending to focus on only one aspect of language, that is, formal grammar. In reality, there is more than one aspect to language as we shall see in 3.5.

► TASK 27

Many structurally-graded coursebooks begin with the structure: 'demonstrative + be + NP' as exemplified by the statement: 'This is a book'.

How many different communicative purposes can you think of for this statement?

The most obvious purpose is that of identifying. This function is much more likely to occur in classrooms (including language classrooms), where learning the names of new entities is an important part of the curriculum, than in the real world. Other functions might include contradicting ('It may look like a video, but in fact it's a book'), expressing surprise ('This is a book? — Looks like a video to me!'), or threatening ('This is a book, and your name will go in it if you don't behave!'). The list could go on.

Matters are complicated, not only by the fact that language fulfils a variety of communicative functions, but that there is no one-to-one relationship between form and function. Not only can a single form realize more than one function, but a given function can be realized by more than one form (see Cook: *Discourse* published in this Scheme).

► TASK 28

Can you think of examples of a single structure fulfilling several functions and a single function being fulfilled by several structures?

In Tables 2 and 3, you will find examples of the lack of fit between form and function. In Table 2 a single form realizes a variety of functions, whereas in Table 3 a single function is being realized by a variety of forms.

Form	Functions	Gloss
	Directions	That's the way to the scenic view.
The cliffs are over there	Warning	Be careful of the cliffs!
	Suggestion	How about a walk along the cliff top?

Table 2

Function	Forms
Request	May I have a drink, please? Thirsty weather, this. Looks like an interesting wine. I'm dying for a drink. Is that a bottle of champagne?

Table 3

▶ TASK 29

What are the implications for syllabus design of this lack of any predetermined relationship between form and function?

The wider view of language, focusing not only on linguistic structures, but also on the communicative purposes for which language is used, developed from insights provided by philosophers of language, sociolinguists, and from other language-related disciplines. The immediate reaction to such a wider view is to contemplate ways of incorporating it into the language syllabus. Unfortunately, the form/function disjunction makes the process of syllabus design much more complex than it would have been had there been a neat one-to-one form/function relationship. We shall look at the practical difficulties of incorporating formal and functional elements into syllabus design in Section Two.

In recent years, criticism of grammatical syllabuses has come from researchers in the field of SLA. Some of the questions addressed by SLA researchers of interest to syllabus planners are as follows:

Why do learners at a particular stage fail to learn certain grammatical items which have been explicitly (and often repeatedly) taught?

Can syllabus items be sequenced to make them easier to learn?

What learning activities appear to promote acquisition?

Is there any evidence that teaching does, in fact, result in learning?

▶ TASK 30

Two important SLA studies carried out during the 1970s were those by Dulay and Burt (1973) and Bailey, Madden, and Krashen (1974). These studies showed that certain grammatical items seemed to be acquired in a particular order, that this order was similar for children and adults, and for learners from different language backgrounds. It also appeared that formal instruction had no effect on the order of acquisition.

What do you think are the implications for syllabus design of the notion that structures are acquired in a predetermined order?

One SLA researcher has this to say on the implications of the research for syllabus design:

Assuming the existence of stages of development, a logical step for syllabus design might seem to be writing these stages directly into a new syllabus. [i.e. ordering the syllabus in the same order in which items occur in the learners' repertoire.] On the other hand, if learners pass through developmental stages in a fixed sequence, then it might seem equally logical to disregard the question of how the syllabus is

written — at least as regards structure — since learners will organise this aspect of learning for themselves.
(*Johnston 1985: 29*)

In other words, assuming that learners do have their own 'inbuilt syllabus', we could argue that the teaching syllabus should reflect this order. On the other hand, we could simply forget about grading the syllabus structurally, because this aspect of language development will automatically be taken care of.

Johnston argues that decisions on whether syllabuses should be sequenced or not can only be settled one way or another by more research into the relative effects of structurally-graded and non-structurally-graded syllabuses. The difficulty for syllabus planners is that they often have to make decisions before the relevant research has been carried out.

Research by Pienemann and Johnston (reported in Pienemann 1985; Johnston 1985; and Pienemann and Johnston 1987) has led them to conclude that the acquisition of grammatical structures will be determined by how difficult those items are to process psycholinguistically, rather than how simple or complex they are grammatically. They illustrate this with the third person 's' morpheme. Grammatically, this is a fairly straightforward item, which can be characterized as follows: In simple present third person singular statements, add 's/es' to the end of the verb. For example, 'I sometimes go to Spain for my holidays' becomes 'He sometimes goes to Spain for his holidays'. However, this simple grammatical rule is notoriously difficult for learners to master. Pienemann and Johnston suggest that the difficulty is created for the learner by the fact that the form of the verb is governed or determined by the person and number of the noun or noun phrase in the subject position. In effect, the learner has to hold this person and number in working memory and then produce the appropriate form of the verb. Thus the difficulty is created, not by the grammar, but by the constraints of short-term memory.

Pienemann and Johnston use their speech-processing theory to explain the order in which grammatical items are acquired. They suggest that structures will be acquired in the following stages:

Stage 1
Single words and formulae.

Stage 2
Canonical or 'standard' word order, e.g. for English, Subject + Verb + Object.

Stage 3
Initialization/finalization. Final elements can be moved into initial position or vice versa, e.g. words such as adverbs can be added to the beginning or end of clauses.

Stage 4

Semi-internal permutation. Internal elements can be moved to initial or final position, e.g. words can be moved from inside the clause to the beginning or end of the clause.

Stage 5

Fully internal permutation. Items can be moved about within a clause.

In Section Two, we shall look at the implications of this hypothesis for syllabus design, and compare the ordering of grammatical elements proposed by Pienemann and Johnston with those of some recently published coursebooks.

There are a number of complications which arise when we attempt to apply SLA research to syllabus design. In the first place, much of this work assumes that we shall start out with groups of learners who are at the same stage of grammatical proficiency, and that learners in a given group will all progress uniformly. Unfortunately these assumptions are not borne out in practice. Another problem which occurs in second language contexts is that learners need to use certain language structures (such as *wh–* questions) almost immediately. These need to be taught as memorized 'formulae' even though they are well beyond the learner's current stage of development. Finally, learners may need exposure to grammatical items in different contexts and over an extended period of time rather than simply at the point when the items become 'learnable'.

In addition to these arguments, there are the general arguments against grammatical grading of content (whether this grading be based on traditional criteria or more recent criteria stemming from SLA research), on the grounds that grammatical grading distorts the language available to the learner. It could well interfere with language acquisition which is more a global than a linear process, different aspects of grammar developing simultaneously rather than one structure being mastered at a time. The arguments against grammatically structured syllabuses are summarized by Long (1987).

At this point in time, then, the direct application of SLA research to syllabus design is rather limited. While the research has shown that the learner's syllabus and the syllabus of the textbook or language programme may not be in harmony, in order to determine its applicability we must wait until the results of follow-up research become available.

In a recent excellent analysis of the status of grammar in the curriculum, Rutherford (1987) suggests that the abandonment of grammar as the pivotal element in the syllabus may be premature. He argues that:

> The critical need for making these [target language] data available to the learner therefore places a special burden upon the language curriculum and, by extension, the language syllabus.
> (*Rutherford 1987: 150*)

In Rutherford's view, the learner needs direct contact with the target language. We know that it is neither necessary nor possible to provide learners with exposure to all target language constructions, and that a major task for syllabus designers is to identify those aspects of the grammatical system from which learners can generate the most powerful generalizations. These structures must be made available to the learner at the appropriate time (a problem, given the fact that learners will usually be at different stages of 'readiness') and using appropriate pedagogic instruments. In effect, what he is arguing for is a view of grammar as process rather than grammar as product. In other words, grammar learning should not be seen as the memorization of sets of grammatical items, but as the raising to consciousness in the learner of the ways grammatical and discourse processes operate and interact in the target language.

At this point, the view of grammar as process may seem rather abstract. However, we shall look at applications of Rutherford's grammar-oriented syllabus in Section Two.

3.5 Functional-notional syllabuses

The broader view of language provided by philosophers of language and sociolinguists was taken up during the 1970s by those involved in language teaching, and began to be reflected in syllabuses and coursebooks. This is not to say that functional and situational aspects of language use did not exist in earlier syllabuses, but that for the first time there was a large-scale attempt to incorporate this broader view of language systematically into the language syllabus. In particular, it gave rise to what became known as functional-notional syllabus design.

Many teachers, on first encountering the terms 'function' and 'notion' find them confusing. In general, functions may be described as the communicative purposes for which we use language, while notions are the conceptual meanings (objects, entities, states of affairs, logical relationships, and so on) expressed through language.

► TASK 31

To check your understanding of the distinction between functions and notions, which items in the following lists are functions and which are notions?

identifying	cause	denying
time	enquiring	ownership
agreeing	greeting	duration
direction	frequency	suggesting
offering	advising	size
equality	apologizing	warning
approving	existence	persuading

Finocchiaro and Brumfit suggest that functional-notionalism has the 'tremendous merit' of placing the students and their communicative purposes at the centre of the curriculum. They list the following benefits of adopting a functional-notional orientation:

1 It sets realistic learning tasks.
2 It provides for the teaching of everyday, real-world language.
3 It leads us to emphasise receptive (listening/reading) activities before rushing learners into premature performance.
4 It recognises that the speaker must have a real purpose for speaking, and something to talk about.
5 Communication will be intrinsically motivating because it expresses basic communicative functions.
6 It enables teachers to exploit sound psycholinguistic, sociolinguistic, linguistic and educational principles.
7 It can develop naturally from existing teaching methodology.
8 It enables a spiral curriculum to be used which reintroduces grammatical, topical and cultural material.
9 It allows for the development of flexible, modular courses.
10 It provides for the widespread promotion of foreign language courses.
(*Finocchiaro and Brumfit 1983: 17*)

► TASK 32

From your perspective, which three of the above reasons might prompt you to adopt a functional-notional approach as it has been described?

3.6 Criticizing functional-notional syllabuses

As we have already seen, the two central issues for the syllabus designer concern the selection of items for the syllabus and the grading and sequencing of these items.

► TASK 33

What do you see as some of the advantages of adopting a functional-notional rather than a grammatical approach to syllabus design?

What difficulties do you envisage for a syllabus designer attempting to address the issues of grading and sequencing from a functional-notional perspective?

Syllabus planners find that when turning from structurally-based syllabus design to the design of syllabuses based on functional-notional criteria, the selection and grading of items become much more complex. Decisions about which items to include in the syllabus can no longer be made on linguistic grounds alone, and designers need to include items which they imagine will help learners to carry out the communicative purposes for which they need the language. In order to determine what these purposes are, in addition to linguistic analyses of various sorts, it is also often necessary to carry out some form of needs analysis. This is particularly so when developing syllabuses for courses with a specific focus.

In developing functional-notional syllabuses, designers also need to look beyond linguistic notions of simplicity and difficulty when it comes to grading items. Invoking grammatical criteria, it is possible to say that simple Subject + Verb + Object (SVO) structures should be taught before more complex clausal structures involving such things as relativization. However, the grading of functional items becomes much more complex because there are few apparent objective means for deciding that one functional item, for instance, 'apologizing' is either simpler or more difficult than another item such as 'requesting'. Situational, contextual, and extra-linguistic factors which are used to a certain extent in the selection and grading of content for grammatical syllabuses become much more prominent and tend to complicate the issues of simplicity and difficulty.

Many of the criticisms which were made of grammatical syllabuses have also been made of functional-notional syllabuses. Widdowson pointed out as long ago as 1979 that inventories of functions and notions do not necessarily reflect the way languages are learned any more than do inventories of grammatical points and lexical items. He also claims that dividing language into discrete units of whatever type misrepresents the nature of language as communication.

▶ TASK 34

Is this a reasonable criticism of functional-notional principles as these have been described by Finocchiaro and Brumfit (1983), or does the criticism relate more to the way in which the principles have been realized in practice?

3.7 Analytic syllabuses

As we have already seen, syllabuses can be characterized as being either synthetic or analytic. In this book, we shall follow Widdowson's lead and consider functional-notional syllabuses as basically synthetic. When such syllabuses began to appear, they looked very similar to the structural syllabuses they were meant to replace. In other words, while the units in such books generally have functional labels, the content itself and the types of exercises which learners were expected to undertake were very similar to those they replaced. Instead of learning about 'the simple past' learners might now be required to 'talk about the things you did last weekend'.

Analytic syllabuses, in which learners are exposed to language which has not been linguistically graded, are more likely to result from the use of experiential rather than linguistic content as the starting point for syllabus design. Such content might be defined in terms of situations, topics, themes or, following a suggestion advanced by Widdowson (1978; 1979), other academic or school subjects. The stimulus for content-based syllabuses is the notion that, unlike science, history, or mathematics, language is not a subject in its own right, but merely a vehicle for communicating about something else.

The use of content from other subject areas has found its widest application in courses and materials for ESP. However, this adoption has had its difficulties. Very often the learner has extensive knowledge in the content domain and is frustrated by what is considered a trivialization of that content. In addition, as Hutchinson and Waters note:

> In the content-based model . . . the student is frustrated because he is denied the language knowledge that enables him to do the tasks set. Despite appearances to the contrary, the content-based model is no more creative than the language-based model. Although communicative competence encompasses more than just linguistic competence, linguistic competence is nevertheless an essential element in communicative competence.
> (*Hutchinson and Waters 1983: 101*)

Dissatisfaction with the content-based approach, as it was originally conceived, prompted some applied linguists to focus on language as a process rather than as a product. Hutchinson and Waters developed a model combining the four elements of content, input, language, and task. The task component is central, and from it are derived relevant language and content.

> The LANGUAGE and CONTENT focused on are drawn from the INPUT, and are selected primarily according to what the learner will need in order to do the TASK. In other words, in the TASK the linguistic knowledge and topic knowledge that are built up through the unit are applied to the solving of a communication problem.
> (*op. cit.: 102*)

In **4.3**, we shall examine in greater detail task-based syllabus proposals.

▶ # TASK 35

What assumptions about the nature of language learning are likely to be held by someone adhering to an analytic approach, in which learners are confronted with language which has not been linguistically graded?

One major assumption is that language can be learned holistically, in 'chunks' as it were. This contrasts with synthetic syllabuses in which it is assumed that we can only learn one thing at a time, and that this learning is additive and linear.

While analytic approaches take some non-linguistic base as their point of departure, it should not be assumed that analytic syllabus designers never use grammatical criteria in selecting and grading content. While some may avoid the use of grammatical criteria, others incorporate grammatical items into their syllabus as a second-order activity after the topics, situations, and so on have been selected.

3.8 Conclusion

In 3 we have looked at approaches to syllabus design which focus on the end product or outcomes of learning. In 4, we shall look at proposals in which learning processes are incorporated into the syllabus design. We shall see that, once consideration of learning processes is built into the syllabus, the traditional distinction between syllabus design and methodology becomes difficult to sustain.

4   Process-oriented syllabuses

4.1 Introduction

In 3 we looked at syllabuses in which the focus was on the grammatical, functional, and notional building blocks out of which courses of various types can be constructed. Initially, it seemed that functional-notional principles would result in syllabuses which were radically different from those based on grammatical principles. However, in practice, the new syllabuses were rather similar to those they were intended to replace. In both syllabuses, the focus tended to be on the end products or results of the teaching/learning process.

We saw that syllabuses in which the selection and grading of items was carried out on a grammatical basis fell into disfavour because they failed adequately to reflect changing views on the nature of language. In addition, there was sometimes a mismatch between what was taught and what was learned. Some SLA researchers have claimed that this mismatch is likely to occur when the grading of syllabus input is carried out according to grammatical rather than psycholinguistic principles, while others suggest that the very act of linguistically selecting and grading input will lead to distortion.

► TASK 36

What alternatives do you see to the sorts of syllabuses dealt with so far?

In recent years, some applied linguists have shifted focus from the outcomes of instruction, i.e. the knowledge and skills to be gained by the learner, to the processes through which knowledge and skills might be gained. In the rest of 4 we shall look at some of the proposals which have been made for process syllabuses of various sorts.

This shift in emphasis has been dramatized by the tendency to separate product-oriented syllabus design issues from process-oriented ones. This has been most noticeable within the so-called 'British' school of applied linguistics, in which the focus tends to be either on process or product, but not on both. (This is despite the efforts of people such as Widdowson, Candlin, and Breen to present a more balanced view. For a useful summary of the range of positions which can be adopted on syllabus design, see the papers in the collection by Brumfit (1984a).)

In **1**, I argued that the planning, implementation, and evaluation of the curriculum should be seen as an integrated set of processes. If such a view is adopted, it becomes unnecessary to think in terms either of a product-oriented or a process-oriented approach. While relative emphases will vary depending on the context, environment, and purposes for which language teaching is taking place, both outcomes and processes will be specified.

Among other things, it was the realization that specifying functions and notions would not in itself lead to the development of communicative language skills, which prompted the development of process-oriented views. Widdowson suggests that a basic problem has been the confusion of means and ends.

> It is not that the structural syllabus denies the eventual communicative purpose of learning but that it implies a different means to its achievement. It is often suggested that the designers of such syllabuses supposed that the language was of its nature entirely reducible to the elements of formal grammar and failed to recognise the reality of use. But this is a misrepresentation. Such syllabuses were proposed as a means towards achieving language performance through the skills of listening, speaking, reading and writing. That is to say, they were directed towards a communicative goal and were intended, no less than the F/N syllabus as a preparation for use. The difference lies in the conception of the means to this end. Structural syllabuses are designed on the assumption that it is the internalisation of grammar coupled with the exercise of linguistic skills in motor-perceptual manipulation (usage) which affords the most effective preparation for the reality of communicative encounters (use).
> (*Widdowson 1987: 68*)

Widdowson's argument here parallels the discussion in **2** on the nature of 'general English' and its implications for the syllabus. There it was pointed out that classroom tasks could be justified, either because they replicated the sorts of tasks that learners would need to carry out in the real world, or because they stimulated internal learning processes. (There are tasks which could do both, of course.) Widdowson argues that pedagogic tasks (i.e. those which would not be carried out in the real world) can be thought of as an investment to be drawn on to meet unpredictable communicative needs.

► **TASK 37**

What assumptions about the nature of language learning can you discern in the above quote from Widdowson?

What are some of the implications of these assumptions for syllabus design?

In **4.2** we shall look at some of the ways in which these ideas have made their appearance as proposals for 'procedural' or 'process' syllabuses. In **4.3** we shall look at proposals for 'task-based' syllabuses.

4.2 Procedural syllabuses

Despite some differences in practice, the principles underlying procedural and task-based syllabuses are very similar. In fact, they are seen as synonymous by Richards, Platt, and Weber (1985), who describe them both as follows:

> . . . a syllabus which is organised around tasks, rather than in terms of grammar or vocabulary. For example the syllabus may suggest a variety of different kinds of tasks which the learners are expected to carry out in the language, such as using the telephone to obtain information; drawing maps based on oral instructions; performing actions based on commands given in the target language; giving orders and instructions to others, etc. It has been argued that this is a more effective way of learning a language since it provides a purpose for the use and learning of a language other than simply learning language items for their own sake.
> (*Richards, Platt, and Weber 1985: 289*)

Both task-based and procedural syllabuses share a concern with the classroom processes which stimulate learning. They therefore differ from syllabuses in which the focus is on the linguistic items that students will learn or the communicative skills that they will be able to display as a result of instruction. In both approaches, the syllabus consists, not of a list of items determined through some form of linguistic analysis, nor of a description of what learners will be able to do at the end of a course of study, but of the specification of the tasks and activities that learners will engage in in class.

▶ TASK 38

Which of the following planning tasks are likely to be most important to a procedural or task-based syllabus designer?
– needs analysis
– specification of real-world learning goals
– specification of linguistic content
– specification of topics and themes
– specification of performance objectives
– specification of learning tasks and activities

One particular proposal which has been widely promoted is the 'Bangalore Project' of which N. S. Prabhu was the principal architect. Until recently, there was relatively little information on this project, but this has changed with the publication of Prabhu's *Second Language Pedagogy*.

> Attempts to systematize inputs to the learner through a linguistically organized syllabus, or to maximize the practice of particular parts of language structure through activities deliberately planned for that purpose were regarded as being unhelpful to the development of grammatical competence and detrimental to the desired preoccupation with meaning in the classroom . . . it was decided that teaching should consequently be concerned with creating conditions for coping with meaning in the classroom, to the exclusion of any deliberate regulation of the development of grammatical competence or a mere simulation of language behaviour.
> (*Prabhu 1987: 1–2*)

> . . . the issue was thus one of the nature of grammatical knowledge to be developed: if the desired form of knowledge was such that it could *operate* subconsciously, it was best for it to *develop* subconsciously as well.
> (*op. cit.: 14–15*)

> . . . while the conscious mind is working out some of the meaning-content, a subconscious part of the mind perceives, abstracts, or acquires (or recreates, as a cognitive structure) some of the linguistic structuring embodied in those entities, as a step in the development of an internal system of rules.
> (*op. cit.: 59–60*)

► ## TASK 39

What assumptions about the nature of language learning are revealed by these extracts?

To what extent does your own experience lead you to agree or disagree with these assumptions?

(For a different perspective, you might like to read Breen (1987), and Somerville-Ryan (1987), who emphasize the role of the learner in process syllabus design. It is also worth reading Rutherford (1987) for a very different view of grammar-learning as process.)

Prabhu provides the following three task 'types' which were used in the project.

> 1 *Information-gap activity*, which involves a transfer of given information from one person to another — or from one form or another, or from one place to another — generally calling for the decoding or encoding of information from or into language.

2 *Reasoning-gap activity*, which involves deriving some new information from given information through processes of inference, deduction, practical reasoning, or a perception of relationships or patterns.

3 *Opinion-gap activity*, which involves identifying and articulating a personal preference, feeling, or attitude in response to a given situation.

(*op. cit.*: 46–7)

► **TASK 40**

During the course of the project, teachers came to prefer reasoning-gap activities over the other two types.

Can you suggest why this might have been so?

What would be the major differences between a procedural syllabus and a traditional grammatical syllabus?

One possible criticism of the Bangalore Project is that no guidance is provided on the selection of problems and tasks, nor how these might relate to the real-world language needs of the learners. In other words, the focus is exclusively on learning processes and there is little or no attempt to relate these processes to outcomes.

► **TASK 41**

Do you think that this is a reasonable criticism?

How important is it for a syllabus to specify both learning processes and outcomes?

Can you think of any teaching contexts in which it might be less important than others to specify outcomes?

4.3 Task-based syllabuses

We shall now look at some other proposals for the use of tasks as the point of departure in syllabus design. The selection of 'task' as a basic building block has been justified on several grounds, but most particularly for pedagogic and psycholinguistic reasons. Long and Crookes (1986) cite general educational literature which suggests that tasks are a more salient unit of planning for teachers than objectives; Candlin (1987) provides a pedagogic rationale, while Long (1985) looks to SLA research (although, as we saw in 3, SLA research can be invoked to support contrary views on syllabus design).

▶ TASK 42

How do you think the term 'task' might be defined by language syllabus designers?

Despite its rather recent appearance on the syllabus scene, 'task-based' covers several divergent approaches. Two recent definitions of 'task' are provided below.

> . . . a piece of work undertaken for oneself or for others, freely or for some reward. Thus, examples of tasks include painting a fence, dressing a child, filling out a form, buying a pair of shoes, making an airline reservation . . . In other words, by "task" is meant the hundred and one things people do in everyday life.
> (*Long 1985: 89*)

> . . . an activity or action which is carried out as the result of processing or understanding language (i.e. as a response). For example, drawing a map while listening to an instruction and performing a command . . . A task usually requires the teacher to specify what will be regarded as successful completion of the task.
> (*Richards, Platt, and Weber 1985: 289*)

▶ TASK 43

A distinction which is not always made in the literature is between real-world tasks (i.e. those tasks that the learner might be called upon to perform in real life) and pedagogic tasks (those tasks the learner is required to carry out in the classroom).

To what extent are the authors of the above statements referring to real-world or pedagogic tasks?

Just as writers on task-based syllabus design have offered different definitions of 'task', so have they adopted different approaches to the selection of tasks. Thus Candlin (1987) chooses to articulate pedagogic criteria for task-selection while Long (1985) advocates a form of needs analysis as the starting point.

Candlin offers the following criteria for judging the worth of tasks. Good tasks, he suggests, should:

— promote attention to meaning, purpose, negotiation
— encourage attention to relevant data
— draw objectives from the communicative needs of learners
— allow for flexible approaches to the task, offering different routes, media, modes of participation, procedures
— allow for different solutions depending on the skills and strategies drawn on by learners

- involve learner contributions, attitudes, and affects
- be challenging but not threatening, to promote risk-taking
- require input from all learners in terms of knowledge, skills, participation
- define a problem to be worked through by learners, centred on the learners but guided by the teacher
- involve language use in the solving of the task
- allow for co-evaluation by the learner and teacher of the task and of the performance of the task
- develop the learners' capacities to estimate consequences and repercussions of the task in question
- provide opportunities for metacommunication and metacognition (i.e. provide opportunities for learners to talk about communication and about learning)
- provide opportunities for language practice
- promote learner-training for problem-sensing and problem-solving (i.e. identifying and solving problems)
- promote sharing of information and expertise
- provide monitoring and feedback, of the learner and the task
- heighten learners' consciousness of the process and encourage reflection (i.e. to sensitize learners to the learning processes in which they are participating)
- promote a critical awareness about data and the processes of language learning
- ensure cost-effectiveness and a high return on investment (i.e. the effort to master given aspects of the language should be functionally useful, either for communicating beyond the classroom, or in terms of the cognitive and affective development of the learner).

▶ **TASK 44**

From the above list, select the five criteria which seem to you to be the most useful for selecting tasks.

What guided you in your choice?

What are some of the things which might need to be specified when designing pedagogic tasks?

Doyle (1979; 1983), working within a general educational context, was one of the first to suggest that the curriculum could be viewed as a collection of academic tasks. He maintains that tasks will need to specify the following:

1 the products students are to formulate
2 the operations that are required to generate the product
3 the resources available to the student to generate the product.
   (*Doyle 1983: 161*)

A similar, though more comprehensive set of elements, is proposed by Shavelson and Stern (1981) who suggest that in planning instructional tasks, teachers need to consider:

1 the subject matter to be taught
2 materials, i.e. those things the learner will observe/manipulate
3 the activities the teacher and learners will be carrying out
4 the goals for the task
5 the abilities, needs and interests of the students
6 the social and cultural context of instruction.

This list is so comprehensive that with a little rearrangement, and the addition of assessment and evaluation components, it could form the basis for a comprehensive curriculum model.

► TASK 45

> What, in your opinion, would need to be added to the list for it to form the basis for a comprehensive curriculum model? (You might like to review the discussion on curriculum in **1**.)

Long, who uses needs analysis as his point of departure, offers the following procedure for developing a task-based syllabus:

> The purpose of a needs identification is to obtain information which will determine the content of a language teaching programme, i.e. to provide input for syllabus design.

> Inventories of tasks that result from the type of analysis described above are necessary for this purpose, but insufficient.
> They are only the raw data and must be manipulated in various ways before they are transformed into a syllabus usable in classroom teaching. The steps in this process are as follows:

> 1 Conduct a needs analysis to obtain an inventory of target tasks.
> 2 Classify the target tasks into task types.
> 3 From the task types, derive pedagogical tasks.
> 4 Select and sequence the pedagogical tasks to form a task syllabus.
> (*Long 1985: 91*)

► TASK 46

> In terms of the process-product orientation already discussed, in what way is Long's proposal different from that of Prabhu?

Long's final step raises the issue of grading, which, as we have seen, is one of the central steps in syllabus construction. Given our discussion on the concept of 'syllabus' in **1**, it could be argued that any proposal failing to offer criteria for grading and sequencing can hardly claim to be a syllabus at all.

▶ TASK 47

What difficulties do you foresee in grading the tasks and activities in a task-based syllabus?

It is generally assumed that difficulty is the key factor in determining the ordering of items in a syllabus. All things being equal, items are presented to learners according to their degree of difficulty. The problem for the task-based syllabus designer is that a variety of factors will interact to determine task difficulty. In addition, as some of these factors will be dependent on characteristics of the learner, what is difficult for Learner A may not necessarily be difficult for Learner B.

▶ TASK 48

Suggest some of the factors which you think might have a bearing on task difficulty.

Most of the applied linguists who have explored the concept of communicative language teaching in general, and task-based syllabus design in particular, have addressed the issue of difficulty, although the factors they identify vary somewhat. They include the degree of contextual support provided to the learner, the cognitive difficulty of the task, the amount of assistance provided to the learner, the complexity of the language which the learner is required to process and produce, the psychological stress involved in carrying out the task, and the amount and type of background knowledge required. (We shall examine the issue of task difficulty in **4.7**.)

The development of process and task-based syllabuses represents a change of focus rather than a revolution in syllabus design. Until fairly recently the preoccupation has been with the outcomes of instruction rather than with the pedagogic processes which are most likely to lead to these outcomes. While any comprehensive syllabus design will still need to specify outcomes, and to provide links between classroom processes and real-world communicative goals, they will also need to provide principles for selecting classroom learning tasks and activities. We shall look at this issue in greater detail in **5**.

4.4 Content syllabuses

In 3 we saw that the content syllabus is yet another realization of the analytic approach to syllabus design. It differs from task-based syllabuses in that experiential content, which provides the point of departure for the syllabus, is usually derived from some fairly well-defined subject area. This might be other subjects in a school curriculum such as science or social studies, or specialist subject matter relating to an academic or technical field such as mechanical engineering, medicine, or computing.

Whether content syllabuses exemplify product or process syllabuses is a matter for conjecture. In fact, most of them would probably be located at the centre of the product/process continuum. I have included them in the discussion on process syllabuses because it seems that the best work being done in the area focuses on process rather than product. (See, for example, the work of Hutchinson and Waters (1983) in ESP.)

► TASK 49

   What might be some of the advantages, as you see them, of adopting
   another subject area as the basis for syllabus design?

By selecting subject areas such as those just mentioned, the syllabus is given a logic and coherence which might be missing from analytic syllabuses which are little more than a random collection of tasks. In addition, the logic of the subject may provide a non-linguistic rationale for selecting and grading content.

In Australia, much of the teaching in adult ESL classes is content oriented. Syllabuses take as their point of departure the skills and knowledge which syllabus planners and teachers feel is important for new arrivals. Units of work thus appear with labels such as 'health', 'education', and 'social services'. While the relevance of this content might seem obvious, many learners are confused by content-oriented courses, thinking they have strayed into a settlement rather than a language programme. In such cases, it is important for teachers to negotiate with the learners and demonstrate the relationship between language and content.

In a recent publication, Mohan (1986) argues for content-based syllabuses on the grounds that they facilitate learning not merely *through* language but *with* language.

   We cannot achieve this goal if we assume that language learning and
   subject-matter learning are totally separate and unrelated operations. Yet language and subject matter are still standardly considered in isolation from each other.
   (*Mohan 1986: iii*)

Mohan develops a knowledge framework which can be used for organizing knowledge and learning activities. The knowledge framework consists of a specific, practical side and a general, theoretical side. The specific side is divided into description, sequence, and choice, while the general side is divided into classification, principles, and evaluation. It is suggested that any topic can be exploited in terms of these six categories, and that the knowledge structure of a topic is revealed through the following types of questions:

(A) *Specific practical aspects*
(particular examples, specific cases within the topic)
1 *Description* Who, what, where? What persons, materials, equipment, items, settings?
2 *Sequence* What happens? What happens next? What is the plot? What are the processes, procedures, or routines?
3 *Choice* What are the choices, conflicts, alternatives, dilemmas, decisions?
(B) *General theoretical aspects*
(What are the general concepts, principles, and values in the topic material?)
1 *Classification* What concepts apply? How are they related to each other?
2 *Principles* What principles are there? (cause-effect, means-end, methods and techniques, rules, norms, strategies?)
3 *Evaluation* What values and standards are appropriate? What counts as good or bad?
(*Adapted from Mohan 1986: 36–7*)

The knowledge framework is reflected in the classroom through activities, which Mohan calls 'combinations of action and theoretical understanding', and which are realized through action situations. Mohan claims that any action situation contains the elements listed in the knowledge framework; that is, description, sequence, and choice, along with the theoretical counterparts of classification, principles, and evaluation. The action situations can be presented to learners through the familiar pedagogical tools of picture sequences and dialogues.

► TASK 50

> Mohan's proposal is yet another example of an approach to language teaching in which the focus is on the development of language through classroom activities which are designed to promote cognitive skills. What parallels are there between Prabhu's process syllabus, and Mohan's content-based proposal?
>
> Do you have any criticisms or reservations about Mohan's proposals?

In a recent review of Mohan's book, it is suggested that:

> One basic problem is the author's assumption that the knowledge structures included in his organisational framework are indeed the relevant structures. What evidence is there that there are three, and only three, relevant practical knowledge structures? . . . a second assumption made in this approach to the integration of language and content is that moving from the practical to the theoretical is the direction most desirable for teaching and learning. Is this direction

best for all learners, or do some learn better when they begin from a theoretical base? The level of maturity of the learner, individual learning strategies and previous learning experience may play important roles in optimal sequencing.
(*Perry 1987: 141*)

4.5 The natural approach

The so called 'natural approach' has been most comprehensively described by Krashen and Terrell (1983). Like Long's task-based proposal, the principles underpinning the approach are claimed to be based on empirical research and can be summarized as follows:

1 The goal of the Natural Approach is communication skills.
2 Comprehension precedes production.
3 Production emerges (i.e. learners are not forced to respond).
4 Activities which promote subconscious acquisition rather than conscious learning are central.
5 The affective filter is lowered.
(*After Krashen and Terrell 1983: 58*)

► TASK 51

Do you disagree with any of these principles?

Consider the principles you do agree with: Do you think we need empirical evidence on these, or are they just common sense?

Do you think that Krashen and Terrell can legitimately claim authorship of principles such as 'develop communication skills'?

For which of the principles would you like to see firm evidence?

Krashen and Terrell develop a simple typology, claiming that most learning goals can be divided into one of two categories: basic personal communication skills and academic learning skills, and that these can be further subdivided into oral and written modes.

► TASK 52

How useful is this typology?

Can you think of learning goals which do not fit the typology?

Do you think that the approach might be more suited to basic personal communication skills or academic learning skills?

The authors of the approach claim that:

The Natural Approach is designed to develop basic personal communication skills – both oral and written. It was not developed

specifically to teach academic learning skills, although it appears reasonable to assume that a good basis in the former will lead to greater success in the latter.
(*Krashen and Terrell 1983: 67*)

▶ TASK 53

Just how reasonable is the assumption that the development of communication skills will facilitate the development of academic learning skills?

What view of language would seem to underly this assertion?

The basis of this approach seems to be the assumption that language consists of a single underlying psychological skill, and that developing the ability, say, to understand the radio will assist the learner to comprehend academic lectures. (You might, at this point, like to review our discussion on the nature of language in **2.2**.)

Another major weakness in the approach taken by Krashen and Terrell is the assumption that learning takes place in a social vacuum, and that social aspects of the learning environment (in particular, the classroom) are irrelevant to what and how learners learn. Such an assumption has been questioned by Breen (1985) who suggests that:

> How things are done and why they are done have particular psychological significance for the individual and for the group. The particular culture of a language class will socially act in certain ways, but these actions are extensions or manifestations of the psychology of the group . . . What is significant for learners (and a teacher) in a classroom is not only their individual thinking and behaviour, nor, for instance, their longer-term mastery of a syllabus, but the day-to-day interpersonal rationalisation of what is to be done, why, and how.
> (*Breen 1985: 149*)

4.6 Syllabus design and methodology

It would seem, with the development of process, task-based, and content syllabuses, that the traditional distinction between syllabus design (specifying the 'what') and methodology (specifying the 'how') has become blurred.

Widdowson takes a rather traditional line on this matter, suggesting that a syllabus is the

> . . . specification of a teaching programme or pedagogic agenda which defines a particular subject for a particular group of learners.

Such a specification provides not only a characterization of content, the formalization in pedagogic terms of an area of knowledge or behaviour, but also arranges this content as a succession of interim objectives.
(*Widdowson 1987: 65*)

He further suggests that the two syllabus archetypes, structural and functional-notional, exhaust the possibilities for the syllabus designer. Both types assume certain methodological practices. The structural syllabus, 'will tend to promote activities which serve to internalize the formal properties of language' (op. cit.: 71). The danger of this type of syllabus is that learners may not be able to use their linguistic knowledge in actual communication. The functional-notional syllabus will promote activities which attempt to replicate in class 'real' communication. Classroom activities thus become a 'dress rehearsal' for real-life encounters.

▶ **TASK 54**

The danger of the 'dress rehearsal' methodology, according to Widdowson, is that learners may not be able to transfer what they have learned to new situations but will only be able to perform in the limited situations which they have rehearsed.

Do you agree or disagree with this view? What evidence do you have for your belief?

To what extent do you think learners can transfer functional skills from one situation or context to another? (Do you, for example, believe that someone who has learned to provide personal details in a job interview will also be able to provide details to a doctor's receptionist? Would such a person be able to provide personal details about their child to a teacher? Would they be able to ask for directions?)

How do these issues relate to the discussion in 2 on 'general' and 'specific' English?

Widdowson proposes the following methodological solution:

[the methodology] would engage the learners in problem-solving tasks as purposeful activities but without the rehearsal requirement that they should be realistic or 'authentic' as natural social behaviour. The process of solving such problems would involve a conscious and repeated reference to the formal properties of the language, not in the abstract dissociated from use, but as a necessary resource for the achievement of communicative outcomes.
(*op. cit.: 71–2*)

▶ TASK 55

Compare this statement to those made by Prabhu, Long, and Krashen and Terrell.

What are the similarities and differences between the various proposals?

What are the implications of Widdowson's view for syllabus design?

▶ TASK 56

Widdowson's view would seem to deny that process or task-based syllabuses, in which the 'how' and the 'what' are intertwined, are syllabuses at all.

Do you accept the dissociation of syllabus design issues from those of methodology?

Do you believe that process and task-based syllabuses represent legitimate approaches to syllabus design?

In contrast with Widdowson's view that process considerations belong to methodology, Breen claims that process considerations (i.e. the means rather than the ends) can properly be considered the province of syllabus design.

> An alternative orientation would prioritize the route itself: a focusing upon the means towards the learning of a new language. Here the designer would give priority to the changing process of learning and the potential of the classroom — to the psychological and social resources applied to a new language by learners in the classroom context. One result of this change of focus would be that the syllabus could become a plan for the gradual creation of the real syllabus of the classroom, jointly and explicitly undertaken by teacher and learners. Such a plan would be about designing a syllabus and, therefore, a guide and servant for the map-making capacities of its users. Primarily it would be a plan for the activity of learning within the classroom group.
> (*Breen 1984: 52*)

4.7 Grading tasks

The issue of grading was touched upon in **4.3**. Here we shall take a further look at the grading of elements in process syllabuses.

Standard texts on language teaching have tended to categorize classroom activities according to the demands they make on the learner. It has generally been assumed that the receptive skills of listening and reading make fewer demands than the productive skills of speaking and writing. Standard treatments of activity types, which are divided according to their principal macroskill focus, can be found in Rivers (1968) and Chastain (1976). For a more comprehensive and contemporary treatment of speaking and listening, refer to Bygate: *Speaking* and Anderson and Lynch: *Listening* in this Scheme. Wright: *Roles of Teachers and Learners* also deals with task types and the sorts of language they stimulate.

The development of communicative language teaching with its focus on meaning has led to the use of more authentic materials. These, naturally enough, contain a range of linguistic structures, which has meant that grammatical criteria alone can not be used as a yardstick of difficulty.

Nunan (1985) presents a typology of activity types in which difficulty is determined by the cognitive and performance demands made upon the learner, i.e. activity type is categorized according to type of learner response (see Figure 1). The typology exploits the traditional comprehension/production distinction and adds an interaction element (recent classroom-based research suggests that interactive language use in which learners are required to negotiate meaning can stimulate processes of second language acquisition).

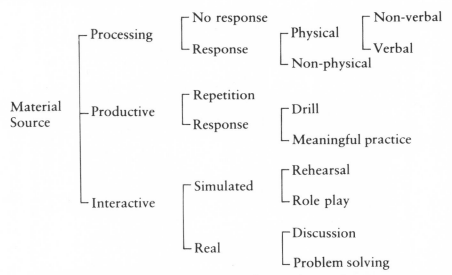

Figure 1: Activity type categorized according to learner responses (*Nunan 1985*)

Using the typology, it is possible to take a given text or piece of source material such as dialogue, a map or chart, a radio weather report, a newspaper article, etc. and exploit it by devising activities at different levels of difficulty. At a basic level, with an aural text, learners might be required to respond non-verbally by raising their hand every time a given key word is heard. Using the same text with much more advanced learners, the task might be to discuss and answer in small groups a set of questions requiring inferences to be derived from the text.

► # TASK 57

How comprehensive is this typology? Can you think of activity types which are not covered?

How useful do you think the typology might be for grading tasks in a process syllabus?

The following example illustrates the way in which a given text (in this case an aural text) is processed at increasing levels of sophistication following the typology suggested by Nunan.

Material Source

Interview adapted from an authentic source

Interviewer: Have you got a family, Doris?
Doris: Family? Yeah, I've got a family all right. My father's still alive. His name's Jack. He's still with us all right.
Interviewer: What about your husband?
Doris: Bert. That's my husband. That's him in the photo, there.
Interviewer: I see. What about children?
Doris: Three, I've got three children. Two sons and a daughter. The sons are Peter and Jack, and my daughter's called Nancy. Nancy's the youngest — she's only eighteen.

Activities

Level 1: Processing

Response: physical, non-verbal
Pre-teach the words 'father', 'husband', 'sons', 'daughter'. Play the tape. Every time students hear these words they put up their hands.

Response: non-physical, non-verbal
Pre-teach the words 'father', 'husband', 'sons', 'daughter'. Students sight read the words on the grid. Play the tape. Every time students hear the words they place a tick in the appropriate box.

father	
mother	
sons	
daughter	

Response: non-physical, non-verbal
Pre-teach the words 'father', 'husband', 'sons', 'daughter'.
Give the students a written gapped version of the text. Play the tape and get students to fill in the gaps.

Level 2: Productive

Repetition
Get students to listen and repeat.
Cue: Have you got a family?
            Have you got any children?
            Have you got a son?
            Have you got a daughter?

Response: drill
Get students to listen and complete.
Cue: Have you got a family (any children)?
Response: Have you got any children?
Cue: a son
Response: Have you got a son?
Cue: a daughter
Response: Have you got a daughter?
Cue: an uncle
Response: Have you got an uncle?
            etc.

Response: meaningful practice
Put students into pairs and get them to ask and answer questions using cue cards.
A Have you got (a/an/any) ——————? family/ children/ son
                                daughter/ uncle/ aunt/
                                niece/ nephew

Level 3: Interactive

Simulated: role-play
Give each student a role card which contains a persona and a family tree. Students have to circulate and find members of their family.

Real: discussion
Put students into small groups and ask them to take turns at describing their families using the structures already practised.

Real: problem solving
Students are given a blank family tree. They are split into three groups, and each group hears an incomplete description of the family.
They work together to fill in their part of the family tree and then join with members of other groups to complete the family tree.

With ESP and content-based syllabuses, an obvious means of grading content is with reference to concepts associated with the subject in question. In subjects involving science and mathematics, there are certain concepts which should logically precede others. Whether in fact such conceptual grading is appropriate for second language learners is another matter, and one which will probably vary from subject to subject. It will also depend on the extent to which the learner is familiar with the subject.

In Mohan's knowledge framework, task difficulty is determined by cognitive complexity. On the specific practical side, tasks which focus on description are simpler than those involving sequence, and these, in turn, are simpler than tasks involving choice. On the corresponding theoretical side, classification is simpler than the identification of principles, which is simpler than evaluation.

Brown and Yule (1983) devote considerable attention to task difficulty. They suggest that listening tasks can be graded with reference to speaker, intended listener, and content.

When listening to a tape, the fewer the speakers, the easier the text will be to follow. Following one speaker will be easier than following two, following two will be easier than following three, and so on. According to Brown and Yule, even native speakers have difficulty following a taped conversation which involves four or more participants.

In relation to the intended listener, they suggest that texts, particularly 'authentic' texts which are not addressed to the listener, may be boring to the learner and therefore difficult to process. They go on to state that:

> . . . it is, in principle, not possible to find material which would interest everyone. It follows that the emphasis should be moved from attempting to provide intrinsically interesting materials, which we have just claimed is generally impossible, to doing interesting things with materials . . . these materials should be chosen, not so much on the basis of their own interest, but for what they can be used to do.
> (*Brown and Yule 1983: 83*)

In considering content, they confess that surprisingly little is known about what constitutes 'difficult' content. The problem here, as Nunan (1984) demonstrates, is that there is an interaction between the linguistic difficulty of a text and the amount of background knowledge which the listener or reader is able to exploit in comprehending the text.

In summary then, a listening text which involves more than one speaker, which is not addressed to the listener, and in which the topic is unfamiliar to the listener will be more difficult to comprehend than a monologue on a familiar topic which is addressed to the listener.

In relation to speaking tasks, Brown and Yule suggest that:

> Taking short turns is generally easier than long turns. Talking to a familiar, sympathetic individual is less demanding than talking to an unfamiliar, uninvolved individual or group. Something one knows about and has well-organised in memory is naturally easier to talk about than a new topic or experience which has little internal organisation in itself.
> (*op. cit.: 107*)

In addition, the text type will have an effect on difficulty. According to Brown and Yule, straight descriptions will be easier than instructions, which will be easier than storytelling. Providing and justifying opinions will be the most difficult. Also, within each genre, the number of elements, properties, relationships, and characters will also have an effect on difficulty, as is demonstrated in Figure 2.

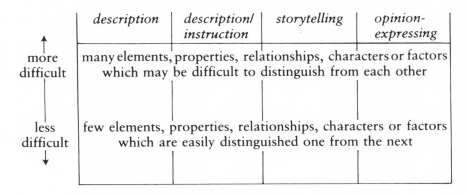

Figure 2: Factors determining difficulty of listening texts (*Brown and Yule 1983: 107*)

Candlin (1987) offers the following factors as likely to be significant in determining difficulty:

— *cognitive load* (the complexity of the mental operation to be carried out; for instance Candlin suggests that tasks which require learners to follow a clear chronological sequence will be easier than a task in which there is no such clear development)
— *communicative stress* (the stress caused by the context, which will be determined by such things as the learner's knowledge of the subject at hand and relationship with the other individuals taking part in the interaction)
— *particularity and generalizability* (the extent to which the tasks follow a universal or stereotyped pattern)
— *code complexity and interpretive density* (the complexity of the language particularly in terms of the sorts of processing constraints described by SLA researchers and the extent to which the learners are required to interpret what they hear or read)
— *content continuity* (the extent to which the content relates to the real-world interests or needs of the learners)
— *process continuity* (the coherence, continuity, and interrelatedness of tasks)

Long suggests that tasks requiring a one-way transfer of information should precede those requiring a two-way exchange, that convergent tasks should precede divergent ones, that tasks in the 'here and now' should precede ones involving displaced time and space, and that intellectual content should be a factor in grading tasks (Long 1987).

One of the most comprehensive treatments of listening task difficulty is that offered by Anderson and Lynch: *Listening* in this Scheme. They identify a range of factors which influence difficulty. These can be attributed either to the listener, the listening material, or the task. The following factors have been extracted from their book (you are referred to the original for a comprehensive treatment of listening task difficulty):

− the sequence in which information is presented
− the familiarity of the listener with the topic
− the explicitness of the information contained in the text
− the type of input
− the type and scope of the task to be carried out
− the amount of support provided to the listener

▶ TASK 58

Review the work of Anderson and Lynch, Brown and Yule, Candlin, Long, Nunan, and Mohan presented in **4** and create your own list of all those factors likely to affect the difficulty of a task.

4.8 Conclusion

We have looked at proposals which focus on learning processes rather than on the end products of these processes. This does not mean that all such syllabuses do not, at some stage, include a specification of what learners should be able to do as a result of instruction. However, if and when grammatical, functional, and notional elements are considered, this happens as a second-order activity.

With the adoption of procedural, task-based, content-based, and other non-linguistic approaches to syllabus design, the distinction between syllabus design and methodology becomes blurred. We shall explore in greater detail the relationship between syllabus design and methodology in **5**.

5   Objectives

5.1 Introduction

It may come as some surprise to those familiar with the theory and practice of syllabus planning to find that we are only now getting around to discussing objectives. I have postponed consideration of objectives until after the discussion of process-oriented and product-oriented syllabuses because the issues raised in those discussions are of particular relevance here. This does not mean that I am advocating the specification of content before the specification of objectives. Whether one moves from a specification of objectives to content and activities or the other way round will depend on the type of syllabus being developed, and the role which the objectives are made to play. In the so-called 'rational' curriculum process (Tyler 1949), objectives are specified before content and activities because their principal role is to act as a guide to the selection of the other elements in the curriculum. As we shall see, in the more interactive approaches to curriculum and syllabus design which have replaced the 'rational' approach, objectives can be useful, not only to guide the selection of structures, functions, notions, tasks, and so on, but also to provide a sharper focus for teachers, to give learners a clear idea of what they can expect from a language programme, to help in developing means of assessment and evaluation, and so on.

In 2, we looked at some of the starting points in syllabus design and at the relationship between learner purpose and syllabus goals.

Goal statements are relatively imprecise. While they can act as general signposts, they need to be fleshed out in order to provide information for course and programme planners. This can be achieved through the specification of objectives. In 5, we shall see that there is no conflict or opposition between objectives, linguistic and experiential content, and learning activities. In fact, objectives are really nothing more than a particular way of formulating or stating content and activities.

5.2 Types of objectives

The term 'objective' is a loaded one which has caused a lot of debate within the educational community. There is disagreement about the nature of objectives and also about the precision with which they should be formulated. Some curriculum specialists maintain that no sound instructional system could possibly hope to emerge from a syllabus in which content is not stated in the form of objectives. Others argue that the process of specifying content in terms of objectives leads to the trivialization of that content. There are, of course, different types of objective, and some of the controversy surrounding their use could well be a result of a lack of clarity about just what is meant by the term itself.

▶ ## TASK 59

Study the following lists of objectives and see if you can identify what distinguishes one list from another.

List 1
— to complete the first ten units of *The Cambridge English Course*
— to teach the difference between the present perfect and the simple past tenses
— to provide learners with the opportunity of comprehending authentic language

List 2
— Students will take part in a role play between a shopkeeper and a customer.
— Students will read a simplified version of a newspaper article and answer comprehension questions on the content.
— Students will complete the pattern practice exercise on page 48 of *Elementary English Usage.*

List 3
— Learners will obtain information on train departure times from a railway information office.
— Learners will provide personal details to a government official in a formal interview.
— Learners will listen to and comprehend the main points in a radio news bulletin.

In 1, the curriculum model of Tyler (1949) was referred to briefly. Tyler's model is based on the use of objectives, and his book was very influential in promoting their use. Tyler suggested that there were four ways of stating objectives:

1 specify the things that the teacher or instructor is to do
2 specify course content (topics, concepts, generalizations, etc.)
3 specify generalized patterns of behaviour (e.g. 'to develop critical thinking')
4 specify the kinds of behaviour which learners will be able to exhibit after instruction

► TASK 60

Which of these ways of stating objectives do you think is likely to be most useful? Why?

What criticisms, if any, would you make of the other methods?

Can you think of any other methods of stating objectives?

Tyler criticized the specification of objectives in terms of what the teacher is to do on the grounds that teacher activity is not the ultimate purpose of an educational programme. He also regarded the listing of content as unsatisfactory because such lists give no indication of what learners are to do with such content. While he felt that the third alternative was on the right track in that it focused on student behaviour, he felt that the specification was rather vague. He therefore suggested that the preferred method of stating objectives was in terms of what the learner should be able to do as a result of instruction. The statement should be so clear and precise that an independent observer could recognize such behaviour if he saw it.

Other proponents of an 'objectives approach' to language syllabus design argue that specifying objectives in terms of teacher activity could result in courses in which the objectives are achieved but the learners learn nothing and that, with objectives specified in terms of classroom activities, the rationale is not always clear (in other words, the links between the instructional goals and the classroom objectives are not always explicit).

5.3 Performance objectives in language teaching

Objectives which specify what learners should do as a result of instruction are sometimes called 'performance objectives'. A good deal has been written for and against the use of such objectives.

In 1972, a book on the use of performance objectives in language teaching was published by Valette and Disick. In the book, arguments similar to those already outlined are advanced for the use of an objectives approach to syllabus design. In particular, it emphasizes the importance of stating objectives in terms of student rather than teacher behaviour, and of specifying input rather than output.

► TASK 61

Complete the following tasks which have been adapted from Valette and Disick (1972: 12).

The following are examples of either student or teacher behaviours. Identify the four student behaviours by marking S next to them.

_____ 1 to present rules of subject-verb agreement
_____ 2 to explain the differences between direct and indirect object pronouns

_____ 3 to write answers to questions on a reading selection
_____ 4 to model the pronunciation of dialogue sentences
_____ 5 to repeat after the speakers on a tape
_____ 6 to mark whether a statement heard is true or false
_____ 7 to introduce cultural material into the lesson
_____ 8 to review the numbers from one to a hundred
_____ 9 to describe in German a picture cut from a magazine

The following are examples of student input and output behaviours.
Write an 0 next to the four output behaviours.

_____ 1 to pay attention in class
_____ 2 to recite a dialogue from memory
_____ 3 to study Lesson Twelve
_____ 4 to learn the rules for the agreement of the past participle
_____ 5 to look at foreign magazines
_____ 6 to attend a make-up lab period
_____ 7 to write a brief composition about a picture
_____ 8 to read a paragraph aloud with no mistakes
_____ 9 to watch a film on Spain
_____ 10 to answer questions about a taped conversation

Most syllabus planners who advocate the use of performance objectives
suggest that they should contain three components. The first of these, the
performance component, describes what the learner is to be able to do, the
second, the conditions component, specifies the conditions under which the
learner will perform, and the final component, the standards component,
indicates how well the learner is to perform. As an example, consider the
following three-part performance objective:

In a classroom simulation, learners will exchange personal details. All
utterances will be comprehensible to someone unused to dealing with
non-native speakers.

The different components of the objective are as follows:
Performance: exchange personal details
Conditions: in a classroom simulation
Standard: all utterances to be comprehensible to someone unused to
dealing with non-native speakers.

▶ TASK 62

Indicate the performance, conditions, and standards in the following performance objectives:

1 Working in pairs, learners will provide enough information for
their partner to draw their family tree. Enough information will
be provided for a three-generation family tree to be drawn.

2 Students will extract and record estimated minimum and

maximum temperatures from a taped radio weather forecast. Four of the six regions covered by the forecast must be accurately recorded.

3 While watching a videotaped conversation between two native speakers, identify the various topics discussed and the points at which the topics are changed. All topics and change points are to be identified.

The specification of conditions and standards leads to greater precision in objective setting, and also facilitates the grading of objectives (objectives can be made easier or more difficult by modifying conditions and standards). However, formal four-part objectives can become unwieldy, with a course spawning many more objectives than a teacher could hope to teach (Macdonald-Ross 1975). One way of overcoming this problem is to specify conditions and standards for sets of objectives rather than for each individual objective.

▶ TASK 63

What do you see as the advantages for language syllabus design of specifying objectives in performance terms?

We have already considered some of the advantages of specifying objectives in performance terms. Mager (1975), an influential proponent of performance objectives, sees them as curriculum 'signposts' which indicate our destination. He rather acidly asks how we are to know when we have reached our destination if we do not know where we are going. (A counter-question might be: 'How do we know where we are, when we end up somewhere other than our pre-specified destination?')

Gronlund (1981) argues that the effort to specify objectives in performance terms forces us to be realistic about what it is feasible to achieve, and that they greatly facilitate student assessment. In relation to this second argument, he points out the difficulty of writing a test if we do not know what it is that we wish our learners to be able to do as a result of instruction.

Other arguments in favour of objectives include their value in enabling teachers to convey to students the pedagogic intentions of a course. (Mager and Clark (1963) carried out an experiment in which students who knew where they were heading learned much faster than students who had not been provided with course objectives.) Their value in assisting with other aspects of course planning such as the selection of materials and learning objectives has also been pointed out.

In recent years, learner-centred approaches to language syllabus design have become popular. In such approaches, the learner is involved, as far as possible and feasible, in the planning, implementation, and evaluation of the curriculum. This involvement is felt to increase the interest and motivation of the learners. It is also felt to be a particularly effective way of developing the learners' learning skills by fostering a reflective attitude toward the learning process (see, for example, Candlin's (1987) list of desirable characteristics of learning tasks in **4.3**).

Advocates of a learner-centred approach to education believe that, at the very least, learners should be fully informed about any course of study they are undertaking. Information (in the learner's home language where necessary) can be provided in a number of forms. It can, for instance, be provided in the form of a specification of course content. One advantage of the provision of information in the form of performance objectives is that these are generally couched in terms to which the learner can relate. If asked why he is attending a language course, a learner is more likely to reply that he wants to be able 'to understand the news on television', or 'to obtain goods and services as a tourist in the target country' than 'to master the distinction between the present perfect and simple past' or 'to use the article system appropriately'.

Proponents of learner-centred approaches to curriculum development also argue for the pedagogic benefits of training learners to set their own objectives (see, for example, Candlin and Edelhoff 1982; Nunan and Brindley 1986). In this context, Brindley (1984) suggests that:

> Setting learning objectives serves a number of useful purposes: it enables the teacher to evaluate what has been learned since terminal behaviour is always defined in terms which are measurable; it means that learners (provided they have participated in the process of setting objectives) know what they are supposed to be learning and what is expected of them; it provides a constant means of feedback and on-going evaluation for both teacher and learner; and it provides 'a way of beginning the individualisation of instruction' (Steiner 1975) since learners can set their own standards of performance and evaluate how well these standards have been attained.
>
> (*Brindley 1984: 35*)

▶ TASK 64

Make a list of the various arguments in favour of an objectives approach as described here.

Which of these arguments do you find most/least convincing?

From your experience, how feasible do you think it is to teach learners to set their own objectives?

What type of learner is most likely to benefit from such an exercise?

What type of learner is least likely to benefit?

5.4 Criticizing performance objectives

Rowntree (1981), a persuasive advocate of objectives during the 1970s, has more recently accepted that there are many ways other than the objectives approach of providing a rationale for a programme or course, and that what may suit one teacher, subject, situation, or student group may be inappropriate to another. His more moderate stance has been prompted by the realization that the setting of objectives is both time-consuming and extremely difficult for many teachers. Shavelson and Stern (1981) also cite evidence suggesting that most teachers simply do not seem to think in terms of objective setting. Despite the difficulties involved, Rowntree asserts that:

> I certainly believe that objectives must be considered at some stage of course planning. If they are not themselves used as the means for arriving at course content, then they can provide a powerful tool for analysing and elaborating content arrived at by other means. (*Rowntree 1981: 35*)

The following lists provide arguments for and against the use of performance objectives.

List A – Arguments against the use of performance objectives
1 It is easiest to write objectives for trivial learning behaviours, therefore the really important outcomes of education will be under-emphasized.
2 Pre-specifying explicit objectives prevents the teacher from taking advantage of instructional opportunities unexpectedly occurring in the classroom.
3 There are important educational outcomes (such as changing community values, parental attitudes) besides pupil behaviour changes.
4 There is something dehumanizing about an approach which implies behaviour which can be objectively measured.
5 It is undemocratic to plan in advance precisely how the learner should behave after instruction.
6 Teachers rarely specify their goals in terms of measurable learner behaviour.
7 In certain subject areas such as the humanities it is more difficult to identify measurable learner behaviour.
8 If most educational goals were stated precisely, they would generally be revealed as innocuous.
9 Measurability implies accountability: teachers might be judged solely on their ability to produce results in learners.

List B — Arguments countering those in List A
1 While opportunism is welcome, it should always be justified in terms of its contribution to the attainment of worthwhile objectives.
2 Sophisticated measuring instruments are being developed to assess many complicated human behaviours in a refined fashion.
3 Teachers should be taught how to specify objectives.

4 Much of what is taught in schools is indefensible.
5 Teachers should be assessed on their ability to bring about desirable changes in learners.
6 Certain subject specialists need to work harder than others to identify appropriate learner behaviours.
7 It is undemocratic not to let a learner know what he is going to get out of the educational system.
8 All modifications in personnel or external agencies should be justified in terms of their contribution towards the promotion of desired pupil behaviours.
9 Explicit objectives make it far easier for educators to attend to important instructional outcomes by exposing the trivial which is often lurking below the high-flown.

▶ **TASK 65**

Match the arguments from List A with the counter arguments from List B. (Both lists have been compiled from a variety of sources which are summarized in Stenhouse 1975: 72–7.)

These arguments were formulated in the context of general education, and those who advanced the arguments were not thinking specifically of language teaching. Stenhouse himself thought that language teaching was one area which could benefit from performance objectives.

To what extent do you think they are relevant to the teaching of languages?

During the 1970s, Raths sought principles for the selection of content which were not dependent on the prior specification of objectives. He came up with the following list.

1 All other things being equal, one activity is more worthwhile than another if it permits children to make informed choices in carrying out the activity and to reflect on the consequences of their choices.

2 All other things being equal, one activity is more worthwhile than another if it assigns to students active roles in the learning situation rather than passive ones.

3 All other things being equal, one activity is more worthwhile than another if it asks students to engage in enquiry into ideas, applications of intellectual processes, or current problems, either personal or social.

4 All other things being equal, one activity is more worthwhile than another if it involves children with realia.

5 All other things being equal, one activity is more worthwhile

than another if completion of the activity may be accomplished successfully by children at several different levels of ability.

6 All other things being equal, one activity is more worthwhile than another if it asks students to examine in a new setting an idea, an application of an intellectual process, or a current problem which has been previously studied.

7 All other things being equal, one activity is more worthwhile than another if it requires students to examine topics or issues that citizens in our society do not normally examine — and that are typically ignored by the major communication media in the nation.

8 All other things being equal, one activity is more worthwhile than another if it involves students and faculty members in 'risk' taking — not a risk of life or limb, but a risk of success or failure.

9 All other things being equal, one activity is more worthwhile than another if it requires students to rewrite, rehearse, and polish their initial effort.

10 All other things being equal, one activity is more worthwhile than another if it involves students in the application and mastery of meaningful rules, standards, or disciplines.

11 All other things being equal, one activity is more worthwhile than another if it gives students a chance to share the planning, the carrying out of a plan, or the results of an activity with others.

12 All other things being equal, one activity is more worthwhile than another if it is relevant to the expressed purposes of the students.
(Raths 1971, cited in Stenhouse 1975: 86–7)

▶ TASK 66

To what extent do you think this list represents an alternative to the use of objectives in specifying content?

The list was written within a general educational context. Do you think the list is applicable to language teaching?

Are some of the criteria on the list more useful than others in your view?

Can you specify these? (Alternatively, you might like to rank the criteria from most to least applicable.)

5.5 Process and product objectives

A distinction which is not always observed by curriculum specialists is that between real-world objectives and pedagogic objectives. (See also the discussion in **4** on the distinction between real-world and pedagogic tasks.) A real-world objective describes a task which learners might wish to carry out outside the classroom, while a pedagogic objective is one which describes a task which the learner might be required to carry out inside the classroom. Examples of both types of objective follow.

Real-world objective
In a shop, supermarket, or department store, learners will ask for the price of a given item or items. Questions will be comprehensible to shop assistants who are unused to dealing with non-native speakers.

Pedagogic objective
The learner will listen to a conversation between a shopper and a shop assistant and will identify which of three shopping lists belongs to the shopper in question.

▶ TASK 67
What is the difference between these two objectives?
Rewrite the real-world objective as a pedagogic objective.

Another distinction which needs to be observed is between objectives which describe what learners will be able to do as a result of instruction (product objectives) and those which describe activities designed to develop the skills needed to carry out the product objectives (these might be called process objectives).

In **2**, we considered the example of the motor mechanic undertaking study in connection with his trade, who might need, among other things, to follow a lecture on the structure and function of carburettors. A 'product' objective for a course for motor mechanics might read as follows:

The learner will demonstrate his knowledge of the parts of a carburettor by listening to a five-minute lecture on the subject and labelling a diagram. All parts to be correctly labelled.

A major problem with such objectives is that they give no guidance as to how the objective is to be achieved. On the one hand, the teacher might make learners perform the terminal task repeatedly in class until they are able to perform it with the required degree of skill. On the other hand, the teacher may wish to focus on activities which do not attempt to replicate in class the terminal performance, but which are designed to develop the receptive and interpretative skills which might be assumed to underly the ability to comprehend lectures of the type described above.

Process objectives differ from product objectives in that they describe, not what learners will do as a result of instruction, but the experiences that the learner will undergo in the classroom. These experiences will not necessarily involve the in-class rehearsal of final performance, although they may do so. The form that the objective takes will reveal the attitude of the syllabus designer towards the nature of language and language learning.

▶ TASK 68

Study the objectives that follow. What do they reveal about their authors' beliefs on the nature of language and language learning?

What are the similarities and/or differences between these objectives and the real-world and pedagogic objectives already described? (Is there, in fact, a difference, or are real-world objectives the same thing as product objectives, and pedagogic objectives the same thing as process objectives?)

1 Students will study the picture sequence in the student's book and ask and answer *wh-* questions regarding location and time.
   (*Adapted from Hobbs 1986: 27a*)

2 Students will study a railway timetable and solve a series of problems relating to departure and arrival times of specified train services.
   (*Adapted from Prabhu 1987: 32*)

The specifications of process and product objectives are not necessarily mutually exclusive. One type specifies the means, the other the ends. It could be argued that any comprehensive syllabus needs to specify both process and product objectives.

▶ TASK 69

Can you think of any teaching contexts in which it would be unnecessary to specify product objectives?

Which type of objective is likely to be most useful to you as a classroom teacher?

5.6 Conclusion

In 5 we have explored the issue of objectives-setting in syllabus design, focusing in particular on performance objectives. Some of the arguments for and against an objectives approach were taken from general educational theory and presented within a language teaching context. In the final part of 5, a distinction was drawn between process and product objectives. In Section Two, we shall see how these ideas have been applied.

Demonstrating syllabus design

6 Needs and goals

6.1 Introduction

In **6** we shall look at some of the ways in which the concepts and processes introduced in **2** have been applied.

6.2 Needs analysis

In **2** we saw that needs analysis refers to a family of procedures for gathering information about learners and about communication tasks for use in syllabus design.

The following sets of data, extracted and adapted from Munby (1978) show the sorts of information which can be collected through needs analysis.

Student A

Participant Thirty-five-year-old Spanish-speaking male. Present command of English very elementary. Very elementary command of German.

Purposive domain Occupational—to facilitate duties as head waiter and relief receptionist in hotel.

Setting Restaurant and reception area in Spanish tourist hotel. Non-intellectual, semi-aesthetic public psycho-social setting.

Interaction Principally with customers, hotel residents, and reservation seekers.

Instrumentality Spoken and written, productive and receptive language. Face-to-face and telephone encounters.

Dialect Understand and produce standard English; understand Received Pronunciation (RP) and General American.

Communicative event Head waiter attending to customers in restaurant; receptionist dealing with residents'/customers' enquiries/reservations, answering correspondence on room reservations.

Communicative key Official to member of the public, server to customer. Formal, courteous.

Student B

Participant Twenty-year-old Venezuelan male. Elementary command of target language. No other languages.

Purposive domain Educational—to study agriculture and cattle breeding.

Setting Educational institution in Venezuela. Intellectual, quasi-professional psycho-social setting.

Interaction Principally with teachers and other students.

Instrumentality Spoken and written, receptive and productive. Face-to-face and print channels.

Dialect Understand and produce Standard English dialect, understand General American and RP accent. .

Communicative event Studying reference material in English, reading current literature, taking English lessons to develop ability to understand agricultural science material.

Communicative key Learner to instructor.

► TASK 70

How useful do you think these data might be for syllabus design? Which information might be most useful in syllabus design and how might it be used?

Do the participants have anything in common?

If these students were studying at the same language centre, would it be possible for them to share part of a language programme?

Would the Munby approach lead to process-oriented or product-oriented syllabuses? Can you explain your conclusion?

Here is a rather different set of data.

Name: (Deleted)
Age: 26
Time in target country: 18 months
Nationality: Vietnamese
Education: Completed primary education
Occupation: Dressmaker
Proficiency: Elementary
Communicative needs: Basic oral communication skills; form filling; timetables; reading signs and short public notices
L1 Resources: Family; home tutor
Learning goals: Communicate with parents of children's friends
Preferred learning activities: Traditional, teacher-directed classroom instruction
Availability: 2–3 × week (mornings only)
Motivation: Brought in by family
Pace: Average

(*Adapted from Nunan and Burton 1985*)

▶ TASK 71

In what ways does the information provided here differ from that provided in the Munby data?

Which do you think might be more useful? Why?

When might the information contained in the table be collected? By whom?

Which of this information might usefully be collected by teachers working in an institution with a set syllabus?

How might the information be used to modify aspects of the syllabus?

What additional information, if any, would you want to collect?

Here are some additional data extracted from the same source.

Name: (Deleted)
Age: 62
Time in target country: 12 years
Nationality: Russian
Education: Completed primary education
Occupation: Home duties
Proficiency: Beginner
Communicative needs: Basic oral communication skills; wants to understand radio and TV; wants to learn vocabulary and grammar; has difficulty with Roman script
L1 Resources: Grammar books; magazines
Learning goals: Wants to mix with native speakers
Preferred learning activities: Traditional, teacher-directed classroom instruction
Availability: Mornings
Motivation: Referred by family doctor
Pace: Slow

(*Adapted from Nunan and Burton 1985*)

▶ TASK 72

In what ways is this second learner similar to or different from the first learner?

Are there enough similarities for both learners to be placed in the same programme?

In designing or adapting a syllabus for this learner, which information would you utilize and which would you ignore?

Which data do you think a syllabus designer with a product orientation might focus on?

Which data do you think a syllabus designer with a process orientation might focus on? What additional data might such a person require?

In **2**, a distinction was drawn between 'objective' and 'subjective' information. We saw that subjective information reflects the perceptions and priorities of the learner on what should be taught and how it should be taught. Such information often reveals learning-style preferences by the learner.

In a major study of learning-style preferences among adult second language learners, Willing (1988) asked 517 learners to rate a series of statements according to how accurately they reflected the learners' own attitudes and preferences. (Interpreters were used where necessary.) Learners were asked to respond according to the following key: 1 = 'No'; 2 = 'A little'; 3 = 'Good'; 4 = 'Best'. The statements to which they were asked to respond are as follows (the statements are ranked here from (1) most to (30) least popular):

1 I like to practise the sounds and pronunciation.	1 2 3 4
2 I like the teacher to tell me all my mistakes.	1 2 3 4
3 In class, I like to learn by conversations.	1 2 3 4
4 I like the teacher to explain everything to us.	1 2 3 4
5 I like to learn many new words.	1 2 3 4
6 I like to learn by talking to friends in English.	1 2 3 4
7 I like to learn by watching, listening to native speakers.	1 2 3 4
8 I like to learn English words by hearing them.	1 2 3 4
9 I like to learn English words by seeing them.	1 2 3 4
10 I like the teacher to help me talk about my interests.	1 2 3 4
11 I like to learn English in small groups.	1 2 3 4
12 I like to learn English words by doing something.	1 2 3 4
13 I like to study grammar.	1 2 3 4
14 At home, I like to learn by watching TV in English.	1 2 3 4
15 I like to have my own textbook.	1 2 3 4
16 I like to learn by using English in shops/trains . . .	1 2 3 4
17 I like the teacher to give us problems to work on.	1 2 3 4
18 I like to go out with the class and practise English.	1 2 3 4
19 At home, I like to learn by studying English books.	1 2 3 4
20 In English class, I like to learn by reading.	1 2 3 4
21 I want to write everything in my notebook.	1 2 3 4
22 In class, I like to listen to and use cassettes.	1 2 3 4
23 I like the teacher to let me find my mistakes.	1 2 3 4
24 At home, I like to learn by reading newspapers, etc.	1 2 3 4
25 In class, I like to learn by pictures, films, video.	1 2 3 4
26 I like to learn English with the whole class.	1 2 3 4
27 At home, I like to learn by using cassettes.	1 2 3 4
28 I like to learn English by talking in pairs.	1 2 3 4
29 In class, I like to learn by games.	1 2 3 4
30 I like to study English by myself.	1 2 3 4

► TASK 73

Which of this information do you think would be most useful, and which least useful in developing a programme for the learners who were surveyed?

What are some of the ways the most useful information might be used in syllabus design?

Which of the statements are designed to obtain information about (1) what they want to learn (2) how they want to learn.

In general, do these learners seem to favour (1) a traditional (2) a communicative (3) an eclectic or 'mixed' approach to instruction?

The learners who were surveyed strongly disliked games and pair work. What would you do if your syllabus were heavily biased toward the use of games and pair work, and you found yourself with students such as these?

In what ways does the distinction between objective and subjective needs analysis parallel that between product-oriented and process-oriented syllabus design?

6.3 From needs to goals

As we saw in **2**, goals come in many shapes and forms. They can refer to cognitive and affective aspects of the learner's development, what the teacher hopes to achieve in the classroom, what the teacher hopes the learners will achieve in the classroom, the real-world communicative tasks the learners should be able to perform as a result of instruction, and so on.

Product-oriented goals can be derived directly from the learners themselves, that is, by asking the learners why they are learning the language. Alternatively, they can be derived by syllabus designers through a process of introspecting on the sorts of communicative purposes for which language is used. These can either relate to a restricted domain (as in ESP) or to the more general purposes for which language is used. The lists of functional items developed by people such as Wilkins and van Ek were the result of attempts to describe and categorize all the different things that users of a language might want to do with that language.

In considering needs and goals, we should keep in mind that the teacher's syllabus and the learner's syllabus or 'agenda' might differ. One of the purposes of subjective needs analysis is to involve learners and teachers in exchanging information so that the agendas of the teacher and the learner may be more closely aligned. This can happen in two ways. In the first place, information provided by learners can be used to guide the selection of content and learning activities. Secondly, by providing learners with detailed information about goals, objectives, and learning activities, learners may come to have a greater appreciation and acceptance of the learning experience they are undertaking or about to undertake. It may be that learners have different goals from those of the teacher simply because they have not been informed in any meaningful way what the teacher's goals are.

Some of the purposes which learners, teachers, and syllabus planners in the Australian Adult Migrant Education Program have articulated are as follows:

— to develop skills in learning how to learn
— to develop the skills necessary to take part in academic study
— to develop an appreciation of the target society and culture
— to develop sufficient oral and written skills to obtain a promotion from unskilled worker to site supervisor
— to communicate socially with members of the target or host community
— to develop the survival skills necessary to function in the host community
— to establish and maintain social relationships
— to be able to read and appreciate the literature of the target culture
— to comprehend items of news and information on current affairs from the electronic media.

► **TASK 74**

To what extent do you think it possible for information such as this to be used to modify a syllabus which has been set by an outside authority?

Would it be possible to develop a common syllabus to meet all of the communicative needs incorporated in the above statements?

If not, what are some of the syllabus elements which might be similar, and which might be different?

Which of the statements could be accommodated by a single syllabus?

For those goals aimed at learners who were at roughly the same proficiency level, it might be possible to identify certain common elements, particularly in terms of grammar and common core vocabulary items. It is in the specification of experiential content (topics, themes, situations, and so on) that differences might occur. The macroskill focus might also vary, with some students wishing to focus on the development of literacy skills and others wishing to concentrate on the development of listening and/or speaking skills.

If learners were at a similar proficiency level, the following purposes could probably be covered by a single syllabus:

- to communicate socially with members of the target or host community
- to develop the survival skills necessary to function in the host community
- to establish and maintain social relationships.

▶ **TASK 75**

Suggest a goal statement which could cover these three learning purposes.

The following nine general communicative goals were developed as part of a curriculum for students learning second and foreign languages at the school level. The goals were not derived directly from learners, but from an analysis carried out by syllabus planners, experienced teachers, and educational authorities.

Instruction should enable learners to:

1 participate in conversation related to the pursuit of common activities with others
2 obtain goods and services through conversation or correspondence
3 establish and maintain relationships through exchanging information, ideas, opinions, attitudes, feelings, experiences, and plans
4 make social arrangements, solve problems, and come to conclusions together
5 discuss topics of interest
6 search for specific information for a given purpose, process it, and use it in some way
7 listen to or read information, process it, and use it in some way
8 give information in spoken or written form on the basis of personal experience
9 listen to, or read or view, a story, poem, play, feature, etc., and respond to it personally in some way.

These have been adapted from the Australian Language Levels (ALL) Project. For a detailed description of the project, see Clark (1987: 186–237).

▶ **TASK 76**

To what extent do these statements represent the sorts of things which learners might wish to do in real life?

How comprehensive is the list?

Are there any omissions or areas of overlap?

Match the ALL Project goal statements with the units from *The Cambridge English Course, Book 1*.

Map of Book 1*

In Unit	Students will learn to	Students will learn to talk about
1	Ask and give names; say hello; ask and tell where people are from.	Numbers.
2	Say hello formally and informally; ask about and give personal information.	Jobs; age.
3	Describe people; tell the time.	Family relationships.
4	Describe places; give compliments; express uncertainty; confirm and correct information.	Geography; numbers to 1,000,000.
5	Describe houses and flats; make and answer telephone calls.	Home: furniture, addresses; telephones.
6	Express likes and dislikes; ask about and describe habits and routines.	Habits and routines.
7	Ask and tell about quantity.	Food and drink; shopping; quantification.
8	Ask for and give directions; ask and tell about physical and emotional states.	Finding your way in a town.
9	Express degrees of certainty; talk about frequency.	How people live; how animals live; weather and climate.
10	Describe people's appearances; give compliments; write simple letters.	Colours; parts of the body; clothing; resemblances.
REVISION	Use what they have learnt in different ways.	Physical description.
12	Ask for and give information.	Personal history: differences between past and present; recent past.
13	Make and grant requests; say where things are; check information.	Shopping; travelling.
14	Ask for and give information.	Abilities; comparison; similarities and differences.
15	Ask for and give information; narrate.	Change; history.
16	Ask for and give opinions; agree and disagree; ask follow-up questions.	Weights and measures; appearances; professions; personality types; dates.
17	Order meals; make and reply to requests; borrow; make and reply to offers.	Food; restaurants; differences in formality; having guests at home.
18	Express guesses; write postcards.	Temporary present actions and states; holidays; change; economics and demography.
19	Plan; make, accept and decline invitations and suggestions.	Travel; distance; going out.
20	Initiate conversations, express interest; ask for, express and react to opinions.	Meeting strangers; frequency; likes and dislikes; being in love; duration.
21	Ask for and give reasons.	Physical qualities; composition of objects; personal possessions; production; imports and exports.
REVISION	Describe; ask for and give personal information; use what they have learnt in different ways.	Comparison; shopping; people's appearance and behaviour.
23	Give instructions and advice.	Sports; position, direction and change of position; cooking.
24	Make requests; ask for and give information.	Hotels; public transport; air travel; place and direction.
25	Talk about plans; make predictions.	Plans; small ads; travel.
26	Talk about problems; express sympathy; make suggestions; express and respond to emotions; describe relationships.	Common physical problems; personal relationships.
27	Narrate.	Ways of travelling; speed; how things are done.
28	Describe objects; narrate.	Education systems; quantity; shapes; parts of things; position; structuring of time-sequences; daily routines.
29	Predict; warn; raise and counter objections.	Danger; horoscopes.
30	Classify; make and accept apologies; correct misunderstandings; complain.	Need; importance; use and usefulness; shopping.
31	Make, accept and decline offers; ask for and analyse information.	Reciprocal and reflexive action; self and others; social situations; possession.
REVISION	Express obligation and opinions; other functions dependent on your choice of activities.	Correctness; other areas depending on activities chosen.

*This 'map' of the course should be translated into the students' language where possible.

(*Swan and Walter 1984: iv*)

How comprehensive is the above list of tasks?

Were there any units which could not be matched with tasks?

The following goals were extracted from a syllabus for foreign as opposed to second language learners of English.

1 To contribute to the intellectual, personal, and vocational development of the individual.
2 To develop and maintain a sense of confidence and self-worth.
3 To acquire the competence to use English in real-life situations for the development and maintenance of interpersonal relationships and to take part in interpersonal encounters through the sharing of factual and attitudinal information.
4 To develop communicative skills in order to acquire, record, and use information from a variety of aural and written sources.
5 To develop mastery over the English language as a linguistic system and to have some knowledge of how it works at the levels of phonology, morphology, and syntax.
6 To increase, through a common language, the possibility of understanding, friendship, and co-operation with people who speak English.
7 To be able to exploit one's knowledge of English to better inform the world of one's people and their concerns, and to be able to participate more actively and effectively in English in the international arena.
8 To foster the development of critical thinking skills and the development of learning skills so that students can continue their education beyond the school setting.
9 To develop the skills and attitudes to listen to, read, and write English for creative and imaginative purposes.
(*Adapted from Nunan, Tyacke, and Walton 1987: 26*)

► **TASK 77**

What are the similarities and differences between this set of statements and the ALL Project goals?

Which goals relate to a product-oriented view of syllabus design and which to a process-oriented view?

Is this list more or less process-oriented than the ALL Project goals?

► **TASK 78**

Study this final set of goal statements.

Participation in learning arrangements should assist learners to develop the necessary knowledge, skills, and confidence to:

1 obtain factual and attitudinal information from visual and print media and to use this information for a variety of purposes

2 interact with others for transactional purposes (i.e. to obtain goods, services, and information

3 develop and maintain interpersonal relationships through the sharing of factual and attitudinal information (e.g. ideas, opinions, feelings, etc.)

4 provide information to others in written form

5 understand the social and cultural nature of living in the target culture

6 develop insights into English as a linguistic system

7 identify their own preferred learning styles and develop skills in 'learning how to learn'

8 continue learning independently once they have left the programme.

For what context do you think these goals have been derived (e.g. foreign or second language learning; adults or children; general or specific purpose syllabuses)?

Which goals relate to language products and which to learning processes?

6.4 Conclusion

In 6 we have looked at applications of some of the ideas and concepts introduced in 2. We have looked in particular at examples of needs analysis procedures and syllabus goals. From these examples, it can be seen that needs and goals can be analysed according to their orientation on the process/product continuum.

7 Selecting and grading content

7.1 Introduction

Here we shall be looking at some of the different ways in which the ideas discussed in 3 have been applied. We shall examine a number of different syllabuses, and explore the ways in which grammatical, functional, and notional items are selected, graded, and interrelated. The aim of 7 is to familiarize you with the ways in which these different elements are conventionally treated. This should provide you with the skills and knowledge you will need to analyse the selection and grading of content in your own syllabuses, a task you will be asked to undertake in Section Three.

7.2 Selecting grammatical components

In 4 we looked at the distinction between synthetic and analytic syllabuses. Synthetic syllabuses were described as those in which content is selected and graded according to discrete point principles. Wilkins assumed that these would be grammatical, but Widdowson has argued that any syllabus which consists of inventories of discrete point items, be they grammatical, functional, or notional, is basically synthetic.

These days, few syllabus designers who adopt a synthetic orientation would be prepared to defend a syllabus based entirely on grammatical forms. Most attempt some sort of synthesis between grammatical, functional, and notional items. Later, we shall look at some of the ways in which syllabus planners have tried to integrate these various components.

We have already noted that there is a lack of any direct one-to-one relationship between linguistic functions, notions, and grammatical forms. While this leads to a certain amount of arbitrary decision-making about which forms to introduce with which functions, some form/function relationships naturally suggest themselves, particularly at lower proficiency levels (for example, 'talking about oneself and others' hardly seems feasible without some knowledge of personal pronouns, copula 'be', and predicative adjectives relating to such things as nationality).

At these lower levels (from beginner through to lower intermediate) most general coursebooks cover items such as the following:

- basic sentence forms
- verb morphology
- noun morphology
- quantifiers
- demonstratives
- definite and indefinite articles

- tense forms
- questions
- negation
- modal verbs
- pronouns

- prepositions
- connectors
- noun phrases, including modification
- adverbials

▶ TASK 79

Match the above grammatical categories with the following items from *The Cambridge English Course, Book 1.*

1 present of *to be*; possessive adjectives
2 *A/an* with jobs; subject pronouns
3 noun plurals; *'s* for possession; present of *to be* (plural); *have got*; adjectives; adverbs of degree
4 *A/an* contrasted with *the*; adjectives before nouns; *on / in / at* with places; *Isn't that . . .?*
5 *there is/there are*; simple present affirmative, *this/that*; *Can/ Could I . . .?*; *tell* +object+ *that* clause; formation of noun plurals
6 simple present; omission of article; *like + ing*; *neither . . . nor*; object pronouns; *at* with times; *by* (bus); *from . . . until*
7 countables and uncountables; expressions of quantity; omission of article; *was/were*; *some* and *any*; *much* and *many*
8 *for* + expressions of distance; *to be* with *hungry, thirsty,* etc.
9 complex sentences; text building; frequency adverbs; impersonal *it*
10 *Have got*; *both* and *all*; *look alike*; *What (a) . . .?*

7.3 Selecting functional and notional components

In recent years, any number of functional and/or notional typologies have made their appearance in the market place. While there are similarities amongst these, as one might expect, there are also differences. This reflects the fact that the typologies have been produced largely through intuition. The following category headings give some idea of the diversity which is possible:

van Ek (1975)
- imparting and seeking factual information
- expressing and finding out intellectual attitudes
- expressing and finding out emotional attitudes
- expressing and finding out moral attitudes
- getting things done
- socializing

Wilkins (1976)
- modality
- suasion
- argument

- rational enquiry and exposition
- personal emotions
- emotional relations

Finocchiaro (in Finocchiaro and Brumfit 1983)
- personal
- interpersonal
- directive
- referential
- imaginative

ALL Project (Clark 1987)
- establishing and maintaining relationships and discussing topics of interest
- problem-solving
- searching for specific information for some given purpose, processing it, and using it
- listening to or reading information, processing it, and using it
- giving information in spoken or written form on the basis of personal experience
- listening to, reading, or viewing and responding to a stimulus
- creating an imaginative text

(*Adapted from Clark 1987: 227–8*)

The authors of these lists imply that they incorporate all of the possible uses to which language can be put.

▶ TASK 80

What are the similarities and differences between these lists?

Which of the above lists do you think most satisfactorily captures the various real-world uses to which your learners might put language? Why?

Are there any omissions? If so, what are they?

7.4 Relating grammatical, functional, and notional components

As we have already seen, the link between grammatical, functional, and notional components is not entirely predictable, although there are certain components which are consistently linked together by syllabus designers and coursebook writers.

▶ TASK 81

This list below contains the functional content from the first ten units of *Checkpoint English* in jumbled order. Suggest the grammatical items which might be taught in each unit.

List A
  1 describing houses
     reminding
     contradicting
     asking for directions

2 giving your full name
   apologizing
   asking for help

3 interrupting politely
   asking for help
   describing oneself
   telling the time

4 identifying
   asking for possessions

5 well-wishing
   inviting, offering
   accepting, declining

6 describing present and future events, activities
   complaining

7 giving your name
   giving personal information

8 offering, inviting, accepting, declining
   checking quantity and quality

9 giving instructions
   expressing possession
   warning

10 making suggestions
    asking leading questions
    making leading statements

► TASK 82

The list below contains the grammatical items taught in the first ten units of *Checkpoint English*. Match these with the functional contents listed in Task 81.

List B

A *Be:* present affirmative
   Subject pronouns
   Here, there; this, that; these, those; my; your
   Indefinite article
   Definite article

B *Be:* present, interrogative, affirmative
   Possessive adjectives

C *Be:* negative, interrogative
   Question words
   Subject, object pronouns
   There is (are)

D Simple present
   Adverbs of frequency

E *Have*
  At, in, on, next to
  Noun plurals

F *Have got*
  In, on, under, near
  Noun plurals

G *Be:* past
  Noun plurals
  Only
  Noun + *'s*

H *Some, any, a lot of, many, much*
  Noun plurals
  Nouns indicating gender

I Regular past simple
  Possessive pronouns and adjectives
  Noun plurals
  Who, who is, who's, whose

J Present progressive, affirmative, negative
  Irregular past

Which, if any of these, did you find comparatively easy to link together?

Which seemed to be arbitrary?

Many of the coursebooks currently available attempt to integrate topical and notional elements as well as grammatical and functional ones.

▶ ## TASK 83

The following lists of functional components (List A) and notional/topical components (List B) have been taken from *The Cambridge English Course, Book 1*. Match the items in List A with those in List B. (When you have finished, you can check your answers against the table of contents in Task 76.)

List A
Students will learn to:
  1 Ask and give names; say hello; ask and tell where people are from.
  2 Say hello formally and informally; ask about and give personal information.
  3 Describe people; tell the time.
  4 Describe places; give compliments; express uncertainty; confirm and correct information.
  5 Describe houses and flats; make and answer telephone calls.
  6 Express likes and dislikes; ask about and describe habits and routines.

 7 Ask and tell about quantity.
 8 Ask for and give directions; ask for and tell about physical and emotional states.
 9 Express degrees of certainty; talk about frequency.
10 Describe people's appearances; give compliments; write simple letters.

List B
Students will learn to talk about:
 1 Home: furniture; addresses; telephones.
 2 Food and drink; shopping; quantification.
 3 How people live; how animals live; weather and climate.
 4 Jobs; age.
 5 Colours; parts of the body; clothing; resemblances.
 6 Finding your way in a town.
 7 Family relationships.
 8 Geography; numbers to 1,000,000.
 9 Habits and routines.
10 Numbers.

Which of these did you find comparatively easy to match?

Which were difficult? Why?

In which of the above coursebook units do you think the following sentences appeared?

 1 Joe and Ann have got three children.
 2 I like the Greek bronze very much.
 3 I don't think that cats eat insects.
 4 There is a fridge in the kitchen.
 5 Sheila has got long dark hair and brown eyes.
 6 Where's the nearest post office, please?
 7 What do you do?
 8 There are seven calories in tomatoes.
 9 Dundee is a town in the east of Scotland.
10 Where do you come from?

Which of these did you find comparatively easy to match?

Which, if any, were difficult? Why?

Which could have appeared in more than one unit? What does this say about the relationship between form and function?

Which grammatical items could these sentences be used to exemplify?

The following extract is taken from the Graded Levels of Achievement in Foreign Language Learning Syllabus Guidelines.

D1 Tasks: conversation and correspondence

Event	Functions and Notions likely to be involved	Examples of Tasks
D1.1 Identifying a person or object Conversation in pairs or in groups	Functions Describing Seeking information Seeking confirmation Notions Size, colour, shape, position, parts of body, clothes, possessions, actions, contents of handbag, etc + Physical and psychological characteristics	Pupil A has a picture of a thief. Pupil B has several pictures and must identify the one described by Pupil A as the thief. Pupil A has a picture of his lost bicycle. Pupil B has several pictures of bicycles and must identify the one described by Pupil A as the lost one.
D1.2 Identifying whether objects are the same Conversation in pairs or in groups	Functions Seeking information Describing Seeking confirmation Notions Size, colour, shape, position, clothes, parts of body, possessions, actions, contents of handbag or suitcase etc + Physical or psychological characteristics	Pupil A has a picture of someone he/she knows. Pupil B has a picture of someone he/she knows. Is it the same person? Pupil A has a picture of a handbag she has lost. Pupil B has a picture of a handbag she has found. Are they the same?
D1.3 Spotting differences Conversation in pairs or in groups	Functions Describing Seeking information Seeking confirmation Notions Objects, people, shapes, position, clothes, actions etc	Pupil A has picture, Pupil B has same picture, with several alterations. Pupils must find the differences without showing each other the pictures.
D1.4 Discovering what's missing Conversation in pairs or in groups	Functions Seeking information Giving information Seeking confirmation Suggesting Giving opinions Agreeing/disagreeing Asking for explanation Explaining Notions Content of squares (as appropriate) Position Sequence Casual relationships	Pupil A has a card: | Bus		
	Airport	
	Air	| Pupil B has a card: | Bus Stop		Port
		Water | They must discuss what they have on their cards and on the basis of this fill in the blanks.
D1.5 Drawing as instructed Conversation in pairs or groups	Functions Giving instructions Seeking information Notions Relevant objects and people shapes, colours, spatial positions, size, sequence	Pupil A has a simple map with plans on it. Pupil B has a blank map and must put in the plans according to pupil A's instructions.

(Clark and Hamilton 1984: 30)

▶ TASK 84

From the above extract does it appear to you that events, functions, notions, and tasks been integrated in a principled way, or do the relationships between these elements appear to be arbitrary?

7.5 Grading content

In 3, we saw that, traditionally, items in a grammatical syllabus are graded largely according to whether they are easy or difficult, and that difficulty is defined in grammatical terms. We also saw that grammatical difficulty is not necessarily the same as learning difficulty.

The two lists which follow set out the order in which verb and tense forms appear in two popular coursebooks.

Cambridge English	*Checkpoint English*
1 Present of *be* (singular)	1 *Be:* present affirm.
2 *	2 *Be:* present interrog. neg.
3 Present of *be* (plural) *have got*	3 *Be:* neg. interrog. *There is (are)*
4 *	4 Simple present
5 *There is/there are*	5 *Have*
6 Simple present	6 *Have got*
7 *Was/were*	7 *Be:* past
8 *	8 *
9 *	9 Regular past simple
10 *Have got*	10 Present progressive affirm. neg. Irregular past
11 *Be* contrasted with *have*	11 Irregular present Irregular past
12 Simple past	12 *Be going to* Present tenses Irregular past

* These sections focus on grammatical items other than verb tenses.

▶ TASK 85

How much agreement is there between these two coursebooks on the order of presentation of verb and tense forms?

What conclusions would you come to about the level of ease or difficulty of different verb and tense forms?

► TASK 86

List and compare the ordering of other grammatical items in coursebooks such as *Checkpoint English*, *The Cambridge English Course*, or *Contemporary English*.

What similarities or differences are there?

What generalizations would you make about the ease or difficulty of different grammatical items?

In **3**, we looked at the work of several researchers in the field of SLA. These researchers claim that the order in which learners actually acquire grammatical items is very often different from the order of difficulty suggested by linguists. Researchers such as Pienemann and Johnston (1987) claim that it is learning difficulty, determined by such things as short-term memory, rather than grammatical difficulty, which determines those items students will be capable of learning at a given stage.

Pienemann and Johnston's theories predict that learners will acquire question forms in the order in which they are listed below.

1 What's the time?
   What's your name?
2 How do you spell X?
   Are you tired?
   Have you got an X?
   Would you like an X?
3 Where are you from?
4 Do you like X?

► TASK 87

Compare this order with the order in which the items are taught in the coursebooks you have examined.

What similarities and differences are there?

Would it be possible to reorder the items in the coursebooks you have examined to fit in with this developmental order?

Would it be desirable to do so? (If you think it undesirable, give your reasons.)

The following lists of functions have been taken from the syllabus guide to *English Today!* Books 1–3.

Book 1

Communicative functions

Greetings, response to greetings, farewell: 1–6, 47
Introducing themselves: 2–5, 26, 27, 30, 32, 34
Asking and telling the time: 48, 49, 50, 51
Counting up to twelve: 36–41, 48–51
Saying the letters of the alphabet and spelling: throughout
Identifying and describing simple objects: 8–23, 40–43, 52–55, 58–64
Simple description of themselves and others: 30, 32, 34, 44–46, 56–61

Questions and answers about personal possessions: 58–61
Asking what things are in English: 9–11, 16–23, 42, 43, 64
Asking a person's name and making simple enquiries: 46, 47
Expressing thanks: 47, 59
Responding to instructions: throughout
Giving instructions: 7, 30, 31, 33, 59
Inability to respond, asking for information: 58

Book 2

Communicative functions

Greetings, response to greetings, farewell: 1–5, 40, 41
Introducing themselves: 2, 3, 26
Asking and telling the time: 23, 31
Counting 1–100: 22, 23, 26, 27, 30, 31, 64–68, 72, 73
Saying the letters of the alphabet and spelling: throughout
Identifying and describing simple objects: throughout
Simple description of themselves and others: 23, 24–27, 37, 43, 52, 54, 55, 63, 78, 84

What people are doing: 56–63, 76, 77
Asking and answering questions about
location: 45–47, 62, 70, 71
personal possessions: 32–35, 38, 43

Asking what things are in English: 9–15, 32, 33, 38, 40, 41, 82, 83
An apology or excuse: 56
Thanks: 35, 75
Responding to instructions: throughout; giving instructions: 43, 48, 49, 56, 57

Book 3

Communicative functions

Greetings, response to greetings, farewell: 1–3, 19, 34, 94
The time: 3, 71, 73; the day and the date: 78–81
Counting: 13
Saying the letters of the alphabet and spelling: throughout
The weather: 82–84, 86
Identifying and describing simple objects: throughout
Simple descriptions of themselves and others: 6–8, 29–31, 63, 67, 73–77, 79, 80
What people are doing: 3, 10, 14, 34, 43, 62
Asking and answering questions about location: 9, 11, 14, 70–33
Asking and answering questions about personal possessions: 15, 39, 62, 63
Asking what things are in English: 37–39, 74, 75

Making simple enquiries about a person: 1–3, 15, 74–77
Asking permission to do simple things: 34, 56
Requesting things needed: 23, 24, 44, 56, 62
Making and responding to an apology or excuse: 3, 21, 23, 62
Thanks: 2, 62
Likes, dislikes, needs and wants: 19–21, 40, 42, 66, 67
Responding to instructions: throughout; giving instructions: 3, 5, 6, 32, 33, 35
Inability to respond: 45
Oral and written prohibitions and injunctions: 32–33, 35, 52–55, 65
Comprehending simple narratives: 19–21, 23–24, 32–34, 40–42, 62–63, 89, 91–92
Recognizing common signs: 52–55
English names of important places: 70, 73

(Howe 1985)

▶ TASK 88

What evidence is there of grading throughout the series?

What principles seem to have informed the selection and grading of items? (For example, has grading been influenced by linguistic, cognitive, maturational, or practical considerations?

As we have seen, the issue of grading is a critical one, and one which will be taken up again in **8** and **9**.

7.6 Conclusion

We have now looked at the selection, grading, and integration of structural, functional, and notional content. The aim of **7** was to explore the ways in which content selection and grading is conventionally dealt with, and to provide you with the skills you need to examine and criticize the selection and grading of content in your own syllabuses.

In **8** we shall look at applications of process-oriented approaches to syllabus design and examine the selection and grading of learning tasks and activities.

8 Selecting and grading learning tasks

8.1 Introduction

We shall now reconsider those issues raised in Section One which relate to the selection and grading of learning tasks and activities. In particular we shall look at examples and applications of the ideas presented in **4**. First, we shall look at the relationship between goals, objectives, and tasks. We shall then look at tasks which have been proposed in relation to the various process-oriented syllabuses discussed in **4**. Finally, we shall examine a range of task types. The purpose of **8** is to provide you with the skills you will need to examine the selection and grading of tasks in relation to your own syllabuses.

8.2 Goals, objectives, and tasks

In Section One, we examined the desirability of relating classroom activities to syllabus goals and objectives so that courses and programmes derived from such syllabuses have an overall coherence of purpose. Failure to provide links between goals, content, and learning activities can lead to a situation in which the desired outcomes of a programme are contradicted at the classroom level. As Widdowson has pointed out:

> . . . it is perfectly possible for a notional syllabus to be implemented by a methodology which promotes mechanistic habit formation and in effect is focused on grammar; and conversely for a grammatical syllabus to be actualized by a methodology which develops a genuine capacity for communication.
> (*Widdowson 1987*)

In **6** we saw that one group of syllabus planners working within a school context came up with the following list of communicative goals:

Instruction should enable learners to:

1 participate in conversation related to the pursuit of common activities with others
2 obtain goods and services through conversation or correspondence
3 establish and maintain relationships through exchanging information, ideas, opinions, attitudes, feelings, experiences, and plans
4 make social arrangements, solve problems, and come to conclusions together

5 discuss topics of interest
6 search for specific information for a given purpose, process it, and use it in some way
7 listen to or read information, process it, and use it in some ways
8 give information in spoken or written form on the basis of personal experience
9 listen to, or read or view a story, poem, play feature etc., and respond to it personally in some way.

▶ ## TASK 89

Match each of the following groups of classroom activities with one of the above goal statements:

A – find the cheapest way to get from A to B from travel brochures
  – listen to airport announcements to find out when one's plane leaves and from which gate
  – listen to alternative ways of making a particular dish and discuss them with a friend

B – read a news item and discuss it with someone
  – read an article and summarize it
  – listen to a lecture and make notes on it

C – write a letter inviting someone to a party
  – determine with someone how best to get from A to B
  – choose with someone which present to buy someone for her birthday

D – make a model
  – lay the table
  – cook something
  – play a game of some sort

E – greet people
  – exchange personal information
  – discuss one's hobbies
  – narrate a recent experience
  – write a letter to a friend

F – discuss the latest news
  – discuss pollution in the atmosphere

G – give a talk
  – write a report
  – keep a diary
  – record a set of instructions on how to do something
  – fill in a form

H – buy food
  – get a meal
  – get accommodation in a hotel

      — hire a car
      — get information about sightseeing
      — write for some information about holidays
I —   read a story and discuss it with a friend

Do the goal statements represent useful headings, or are they redundant?

What purpose, if any, is served by grouping learning tasks and activities under goal statements such as those above?

In 5 we looked at the advantages and disadvantages of specifying objectives in performance terms. It was suggested by some syllabus designers that performance objectives could be useful in certain types of syllabus design because they provided a specification of what learners should be able to do as a result of instruction. The objectives can be specified, either in real-world or classroom terms, and can provide a link between classroom activities and general goals.

► TASK 90

See whether you can write objectives for each of the classroom activities described in Task 89.

Which of these relate to real-world performance, which to classroom performance and which, if any, to both real-world and classroom performance?

Did you have any difficulty writing objectives for any of the activities? If so, which? Can you say why you had difficulty?

8.3 Procedural syllabuses

Certain approaches to syllabus design begin, not with a needs analysis or a statement of goals and objectives, but with lists of classroom tasks. As we saw, there can be problems with this approach: it is often difficult to see how the classroom tasks are related to learners' purposes, and the lists themselves may remain just that, unco-ordinated lists of tasks. The advantage of having a restricted set of goal statements is that it can provide a degree of coherence which may otherwise be lacking. It also enables the syllabus planner to link classroom tasks to the real-world uses to which learners might wish to put their second language skills.

There are, however, circumstances in which it is impossible to derive communicative goals from learners' purposes because the learners have no purpose beyond, perhaps, passing a public examination. In some foreign language teaching situations it may only be possible to make goal statements in vague or even vacuous terms.

In educational contexts where there is no specific communicative end in sight, proposals have been made for basing the syllabus, not on content, but on procedures which are felt to promote second language acquisition. One such proposal is the Bangalore Project.

We saw in **4** that the Bangalore Project has received a good deal of publicity. The following sample tasks are from the Project. Task A has been adapted from Brumfit (1984), while Task B has been taken from Prabhu (1987).

Task A

Appendix: Bangalore exercise (see page 104)

(Prabhu, 1982: Lesson 183: 26 August 1981)

The following dialogue is handed out and read aloud by two sets of students, each taking a part.

Suresh: Daddy, when will the train come?
Rajan: In about ten minutes. It is only 4.10 pm now.
Suresh: Will it leave the station at once?
Rajan: No Suresh, it will stop here for 10 minutes. It leaves Madras only at 4.30 pm.
Radha: Does it reach Hyderabad by 7.00 am?
Rajan: No, only at 8.30 am. We must have our breakfast in the train.
Suresh: How much did you pay for the tickets, Daddy?
Rajan: I paid Rs 360.00 for three first class tickets. When we come back from Hyderabad, we shall travel by second class.
Radha: Yes. A second-class ticket costs only Rs 50/–.
Suresh: Are we going to stay at Hotel Annapurna this time too, Mummy?
Radha: Yes dear, the rooms are very comfortable there.
Rajan: And the food is also good.
Radha: When do we come back to Madras?
Rajan: After a week. We will be back here at the Central Station on Saturday, the 22nd of August.
Suresh: Today is also a Saturday. Our school has holidays for a week from today.
Radha: There is the train! Suresh, take this bag. I'll take this suitcase. Daddy can take the bigger suitcase. We must find our compartment.

Pre-task: The teacher discusses with the class the following questions:

1   Who is Suresh?
2   What is his father's name?
3   Who is Radha?
4   Where are they now?
5   What is the name of the station?
6   What are they doing there?
7   Where are they going?
8   At what time does the train leave Madras?
9   How long does it take to reach Hyderabad?
10 Is it a night train or a day train?
11 Where will they stay in Hyderabad?
12 Will they have breakfast at Hotel Annapurna tomorrow?
13 Does Rajan like to stay at Annapurna? How do you know?
14 Why does Radha like Hotel Annapurna?

---

15 For how many days will they stay at Hyderabad?
16 On which day are they leaving Madras?
17 Will Suresh miss his classes?
18 What luggage do they have?
19 Are they rich? How do you know?
20 How much does a first class ticket cost?
21 How much will they spend for their return from Hyderabad to Madras?
22 The Hyderabad Express leaves Hyderabad at 4.00 pm. When does it reach Madras?
23 Last week Rajan went to Hyderabad. He travelled by second class both ways. How much did he spend on the train tickets?
24 Is this the first time that they are going to Hyderabad? How do you know?

Task: Pupils are asked to answer the following questions overnight.

Say whether the following statements are true or false; give reasons for your answers.
1 Mr Rajan always travels by first class.
2 There are no good hotels in Hyderabad.
3 The Rajans reached the station before the train arrived.
4 Radha can attend her friend's wedding at Hyderabad on 20th August.
5 Suresh was at Madras on Independence Day.

Comment: Pupils' performance, marked out of 10, was:

Marks	*Pupils*
9–10	9
7–8	10
5–6	3
3–4	0
1–2	1
	23

Pupils are now beginning to try to state reasons in their 'own words' instead of merely citing lines from the text.

(*Brumfit 1984: 145–6*)

Task B

2 Instructions to draw

A sequence of lessons based on instructions to draw contained the following task (following a similar pre-task) representing an appropriate challenge at one stage of project teaching:

a Draw a line, from left to right.
b Write B at the right end of the line, and A at the left end.
c Draw another line below AB.
d Write D at its left end and C at its right end.
e Join BD.

When the sequence was resumed two weeks later, with twelve lessons on other task-types intervening, the following task proved to be appropriately challenging for the class. (The pre-task which preceded it introduced conventions such as that 'continue AB' meant continuing the line concerned in the direction of B to about twice its original length.)

a Name the top corners of the square: B on the left and C on the right.
b Name the corners at the bottom: D on the right and A on the left.
c Continue AB and call the end of the line E.
d Continue CD and write F at the end of the line.
e Join EC.
f What should be joined next?

Returning to the drawing sequence a long time later (when about 200 lessons had intervened, though only three of them had been on drawing instructions) the teacher found the class able to do the following task with about the same measure of success:

a Draw two parallel, horizontal lines. Let them be about four inches long.
b Join the ends of the two lines on the left, with a short vertical line.
c Use two parallel, vertical lines to join the right ends of the horizontal lines.
d Mark the mid-points of the parallel, vertical lines.
e Draw a dotted line, horizontally, passing through the mid-points of the parallel vertical lines and extending to the right for about half an inch.
f Use straight lines to join the right end of the dotted line with the right ends of the two horizontal parallel lines.

(*Prabhu 1987b: 33–4*)

► TASK 91

What sort of skills are likely to be developed from tasks such as these?
In what ways do the tasks differ from 'traditional' language tasks? In what ways are they the same?

The Bangalore syllabus does not focus explicitly on language and does not specify the grammatical, functional, or notional items to be taught. Would it be (1) possible (2) useful to specify the grammatical, functional, and notional items which could be taught through these two tasks? If so, list these.

8.4 The natural approach

In **4**, we saw that the authors of the natural approach divide language goals into basic personal communication skills (oral and written) and academic learning skills (oral and written).

► TASK 92

Indicate to which goal they belong, by placing the appropriate letter (A, B, C, D) against each of the tasks that follow the language goals.

Goals
A basic personal communication skills: oral
B basic personal communication skills: written
C academic learning skills: oral
D academic learning skills: written

Tasks
 1 read textbooks
 2 present a class report
 3 listen to a lecture
 4 read and write notes to friends or workers
 5 read signs, including instructions
 6 read and fill out forms (applications and other documents)
 7 participate in a conversation with one or more speakers of L2
 8 write reports, essays
 9 read and discuss literature
10 listen to a conversation between other speakers
11 listen to announcements in public places
12 read advertisements (windows, newspapers, magazines)
13 listen to a film or other audiovisual presentation with academic content
14 study for and take an exam
15 take notes in class
16 request information in public places
17 listen to and participate in panel and classroom discussions

18 read and write personal letters
19 listen to radio, television, films, music
20 read for pleasure

Would learners take part in these activities inside or outside the language class?

Which activities could be part of both a language course and a non-language course?

Krashen and Terrell (1983) suggest that basic personal oral communication goals, for which the approach is best suited, can be expressed in terms of the situations in which students must use the target language and the topics of communication. In other words, they are assuming a link between classroom activities and the real world. The following example is taken from their book:

Recreation and leisure activities
Topics
1. Favourite activities
2. Sports and games
3. Climate and seasons
4. Weather
5. Seasonal activities
6. Holiday activities
7. Parties
8. Abilities
9. Cultural and artistic interests

Situations
1. Playing games, sports

► # TASK 93

Complete the table overleaf, by providing appropriate topics or situations.

For what type of learners would the topics and situations in the table be most suitable (beginning/intermediate/advanced learner; ESL/EFL learner; new arrival/long-term resident of target community)?

What criticisms would you make of a syllabus outline based only on topics and situations?

Area	Topics	Situations
Family, friends, activities	Family and relatives Physical states Emotional states Daily activities Holiday and vacation activities Pets	Birthday party _____ _____ _____ _____
Plans, obligations, and careers	_____ _____ _____ _____ _____	Job interview Talking on the job
Residence	Place of residence Rooms of a house Furniture and household items Activities at home Amenities	_____ _____ _____ _____ _____ _____
Health, illness, and emergencies	_____ _____ _____ _____	Visit to Dr At hospital Buying medicine

Table 4

8.5 Content-based syllabuses

In **4** we looked at syllabuses based on experiential content, focusing in particular on the work of Mohan. Mohan's knowledge framework, consisting of a practical aspect and a theoretical aspect was described. Here, we shall look at ways in which this knowledge framework is realized through action situations.

One of the techniques suggested by Mohan for representing action situations is through flowcharts. The figure on the facing page shows the flowchart of a shopping situation between a clerk and a shopper.

▶ TASK 94

Suggest ways in which the flowchart might be used as the basis of lesson sequences.

Do you think the flowchart could be used for a whole unit or module, or would it only serve for a single lesson?

How might the flowchart relate to Mohan's knowledge framework?

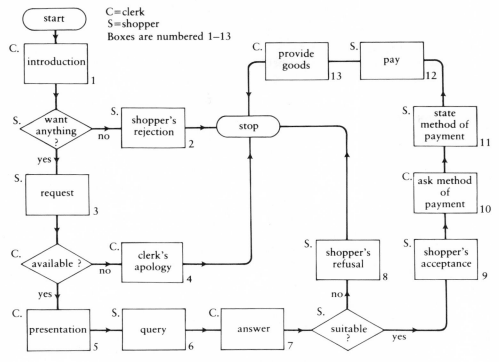

Figure 3:   Flowchart of shopping situation
(*Mohan 1986: 59*)

Mohan suggests that the flowchart can represent situational language and situational content in combination more adequately than can cartoon strips or picture sequences. In addition, the various branches of the flowchart offer alternative pathways which are not possible with linear sequences. They thus relate to the knowledge framework by providing teachers with the potential for developing activities focusing on either description, sequence, or choice.

▶ TASK 95

Suggest some classroom activities for a shopping situation involving description, sequence, and choice.

The following suggestions are provided by Mohan:

Description

Basis: a typical situation includes participants, actions, objects, and a scene or setting. Dramatization or pictures show these visually. All can be described by the teacher.

Examples: shopper gives an identifying description of the item wanted. Shopper and clerk compare and contrast items.

Classroom activity: learners role play shopper and clerk using labels, advertisements, and catalogue descriptions of goods for information. More generally, a description of the state of affairs at any point in the situation gives a starter for role playing the remainder of the situation.

Sequence

Basis: a typical situation is a series of related events and actions on a time line. If there is no discourse we have a chain of actions. With discourse we have a script. These events and actions can be narrated by the teacher.

Example: the clerk's attention is distracted and the shopper leaves with the goods, mistakenly thinking they have been paid for. The clerk calls the shopper back and they clear up the mistake, establishing the chronological order of events and the reasons for the confusion.

Classroom activity: an extension of the above. The shopper is to be accused of shoplifting. Students create the events which led up to this. Then some take the roles of shopper, clerk, and floorwalker and the rest act as the supervisor and interview the others about what happened. A report on the incident is written combining the interview information. Simpler activities include narrating the script or action chain and issuing instructions to the shopper or clerk.

Choice

Basis: a typical situation will include intentional actions. Any such action springs from a choice which derives from a decision situation (some choices, of course, are more trivial than others). The decision situation can be stated by the teacher.

Example: the shopper makes a decision to buy or not to buy. This can be by internal deliberation or by discussion. A possible choice can be offered by a proposal and can be rejected with a refutation. Alternatives can be compared and contrasted and their consequences explored.

Classroom activity: the main decision is whether to buy or not. The students create the decision situation that this springs from. This can be simpler or more complex, depending on the level of the students. A statement of the decision situation is the basis for a problem solving activity.

(*Extracted from Mohan 1986: 65–6*)

▶ # TASK 96

Select some other action situation and develop it in the same way as Mohan developed the shopping situation.

If content-based syllabuses consisted of nothing more than a series of action situations strung together, they could be criticized for being incomplete. In the following task you are asked to consider some of the additional elements which might be specified.

▶   # TASK 97

For what types of students might the shopping situation be appropriate?

To which real-world tasks might it relate?

Specify a given learner proficiency level, and suggest performance objectives for the shopping situation.

Suggest grammatical, functional, and notional components.

What principles do you think might guide the selection of content in a content-based syllabus? Will they be basically the same as or different from those guiding content selection in other analytic syllabuses we have looked at?

What principles might be invoked in grading content? Will these be basically the same as or different from those used to grade content in other analytic syllabuses?

8.6 Levels of difficulty

As we have already seen, grading becomes a major problem in syllabuses based on tasks and activities rather than lists of grammatical items.

In **4.7** the comments by Brown and Yule on task difficulty were discussed, and you were asked to produce a list of factors likely to influence task difficulty.

The following tasks have been adapted from Brown and Yule. In each task, the students are working in pairs.

1 Both students have a photograph which is almost identical. The speaker has to describe what is in the photograph as accurately as possible in order that the listener can identify in what way his photograph differs from the one which the speaker is describing.

2 The speaker has a diagram. The listener has a blank sheet of paper, a black pen, and a red pen. The speaker has to instruct the listener to reproduce the diagram as accurately as possible on his sheet of paper. The listener has to listen carefully and to follow the speaker's instructions.

3 The speaker has a cartoon strip story. The listener has a set of pictures which show scenes or the characters from the story and some from different stories. The speaker has to tell the story so that the listener will be able to identify which scenes or characters fit the account he hears.

4 The speaker has a set of photographs depicting a sequence of events leading up to a car crash. The listener has a set of photographs, some of

which show details of the particular car crash being described and some for another car crash. Alternatively, the listener has a road layout design on which he has to draw the locations and movements of the cars involved in the crash.

5 The learner watches a short piece of video film in which a teacher expresses a fairly strong opinion that corporal punishment is necessary in school to ensure that teachers can do their work and that students can learn. Learners are asked to watch the film and say what they think about the matter.

► TASK 98

Refer to the list of factors likely to determine task difficulty that you worked on in Task 58 and grade the above tasks from easiest to most difficult.

It has been suggested that, all things being equal, activities which can be exploited at different levels of difficulty are more useful than those which are only suitable for a single proficiency level. Such activities are obviously extremely useful in mixed-ability classrooms.

Because of the variety of factors involved, it is not always easy to determine whether a given activity is easier or more difficult than another; it is sometimes a matter of judgement.

The following activities have been extracted from a book designed for mixed-ability groups. Tasks at different levels of difficulty have been derived from the same piece of data (in this instance an airport announcement).

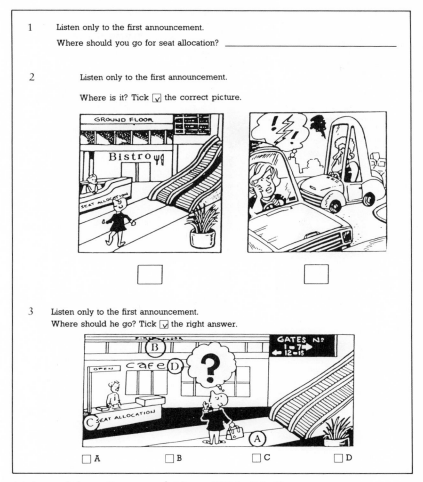

1 Listen only to the first announcement.
Where should you go for seat allocation? _____

2 Listen only to the first announcement.
Where is it? Tick ☑ the correct picture.

3 Listen only to the first announcement.
Where should he go? Tick ☑ the right answer.

☐ A   ☐ B   ☐ C   ☐ D

(*Adapted from Jones and Moar 1985: 25–9*)

▶ TASK 99

Study the above activities and decide which is the easiest and which the most difficult.

An alternative to the procedure adopted by Jones and Moar is to devise activities which can be worked on in small groups, where each learner can contribute according to his/her level of competence. One commonly used activity which lends itself well to mixed-ability groups consists of a series of pictures depicting a narrative. Each student is given a picture. The task is for each student to describe his/her picture and then for the group as a whole to decide on the appropriate order in which the pictures should be sequenced.

The following unit extract is from the *Challenges* coursebook.

Searching and Sharing

BBC/Challenges Research Notes

CHARLOTTE

Charlotte is 18 years old and works as a receptionist in Oxford Street in London's West End. She is a pretty girl with a lively personality. She gets on well with people and has a lot of friends.

At present, Charlotte has no fixed address. She has been looking for somewhere to live for about three months. So far she has been unsuccessful and has been sleeping on the floor of a friend's flat.

Charlottes's parents live in the country just outside London and although it is possible to live at home with her parents and commute to London every day to work like thousands of other people, Charlotte wants to be independent. She wants to lead a life of her own.

Charlotte's boyfriend, Glen, shares a flat with three other friends. They were lucky. They found a flat very quickly. Charlotte, however, has not been so lucky.

Every day she buys an evening paper and looks through the advertisements. She visits and telephones Flat Agencies about three times a week. She buys a magazine called 'Time Out' every Thursday and looks through the 'Flats to Share' pages very carefully.

She has been to see a number of different places in different parts of London. Each time she has been disappointed for one reason or another.

STEP 1 READING

STEP 2 QUESTIONNAIRE

You are the person who interviews Charlotte at a flat agency. Fill in the form for her using the information in the text.

AROUND TOWN AGENCY

CLIENT'S DETAILS   CONFIDENTIAL

1. Name of client _____
2. Age of client _____
3. Occupation _____
4. Present address _____
5. Kind of accommodation wanted _____
6. Preferred location (In London/Out of town): _____
7. How long has the client been looking for new accommodation? _____
8. How has the client been looking for accommodation? _____
9. If the client is looking for shared accommodation write a brief note on his/her personality _____

STEP 3 WRITING

Tell the story of Charlotte's search. Fill in the gaps using a suitable form of the words in brackets.

When Charlotte left home she .... (go) to stay with friends in London. She first .... (consult) an agent. Then she .... (visit) a flat which a 50-year-old woman .... (want) to share. The following morning she .... (phone) about another room. When she .... (get) there, she .... (find) that the room was very tiny. And she .... (not like) the girl there. She ... . (call at) another flat, but she was too late. They had found someone. Next she .... (ring) a boy who lived in a bed-sitter. But the bed-sitter .... (not suit) her either. She .... (begin) to feel very depressed. Then a friend .... (read) her an advertisement from the newspaper. The people .... (want) someone to share a relaxed, happy flat. Charlotte .... (phone) them. The girls .... (interview) her and another girl. They .... (choose) Charlotte. The next Saturday she .... (move in).

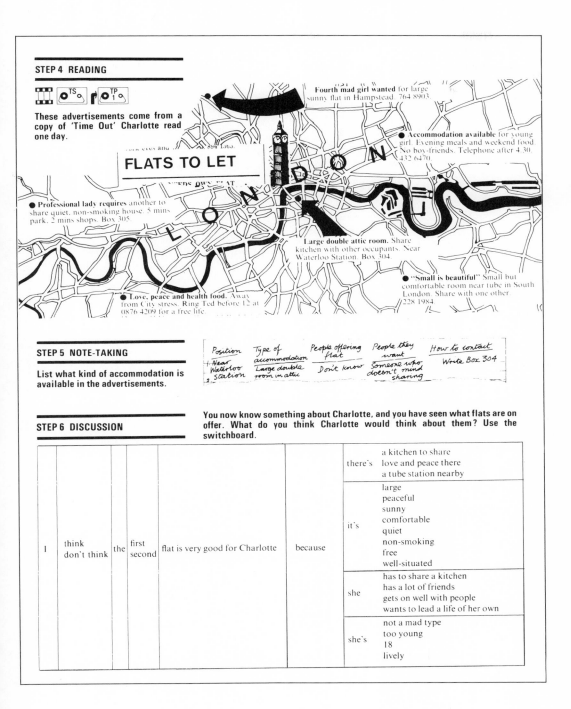

STEP 4 READING

These advertisements come from a copy of 'Time Out' Charlotte read one day.

FLATS TO LET

● **Fourth mad girl wanted** for large sunny flat in Hampstead. 764 8903.

● **Accommodation available** for young girl. Evening meals and weekend food. No boy-friends. Telephone after 4.30. 432 6470.

● **Professional lady requires** another to share quiet, non-smoking house. 5 mins park. 2 mins shops. Box 305.

● **Large double attic room.** Share kitchen with other occupants. Near Waterloo Station. Box 304.

● **"Small is beautiful"** Small but comfortable room near tube in South London. Share with one other. 228 1984.

● **Love, peace and health food.** Away from City stress. Ring Ted before 12 at 0876 4209 for a free life.

STEP 5 NOTE-TAKING

List what kind of accommodation is available in the advertisements.

Position	Type of accommodation	People offering flat	People they want	How to contact
1 Near Waterloo 2 Station	Large double room in attic	Don't know	Someone who doesn't mind sharing	Write Box 304

STEP 6 DISCUSSION

You now know something about Charlotte, and you have seen what flats are on offer. What do you think Charlotte would think about them? Use the switchboard.

I	think / don't think	the	first / second	flat is very good for Charlotte	because	there's	a kitchen to share / love and peace there / a tube station nearby
						it's	large / peaceful / sunny / comfortable / quiet / non-smoking / free / well-situated
						she	has to share a kitchen / has a lot of friends / gets on well with people / wants to lead a life of her own
						she's	not a mad type / too young / 18 / lively

TASK 1

Now tell your group what you think about the flats.

I	like don't like prefer	the	first second	flat	because	I'm .... it's .... there's .... there isn't ....

TASK 2

You have arrived in an English-speaking country. You are looking for a flat, perhaps alone, perhaps to share with somebody. Write an advertisement for the newspaper asking for accommodation. Your advertisement might look something like these:

> FOREIGN STUDENT, man, 30 years old, seeks flat to share, preferably with Englishman, Town Centre. Cooking facilities essential. Write Box No. 789.

Please insert my small ad for   week(s) in the   section of CLASSIFIED First insert date to be.   If received too late for publication on this day, please insert my ad. in the following edition YES NO

French	girl,	studying	at
University,	needs	small	flat
for	next	January.	Sitting
room,	Bedroom,	Bathroom,	Kitchen.
Maximum	– £25	a	week.
Phone	42709		

(Abbs, Candlin, Edelhoff, Moston, and Sexton 1979: 2–4)

▶ ## TASK 100

Do the above activities seem to be sequenced in any principled way?

If so, what criteria have been utilized in sequencing the activities?

Does task difficulty seem to be one of the factors influencing the sequencing of tasks?

What are the factors determining the difficulty of the different tasks in the unit?

The sample unit extracts which follow have been taken from Hutchinson and Waters (1983).

Unit 1: Tools

Look at the pictures in the Input below and make a list of <u>all</u> the tools and materials you would need for the job.

<u>INPUT</u>   Replacing a pane

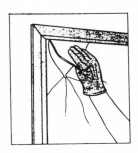

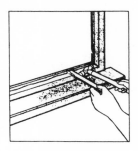

1. Remove the broken pane, wearing gloves and taking great care.

2. Scrape away the old putty with a hammer and a suitable tool.

3. Take out any window pins left in the frame.

4. Brush off all dust and clean remaining putty from the frame.

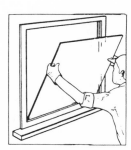

5. Take diagonal as well as horizontal and vertical measurements.

6. Carefully ease the new pane into position, wearing gloves.

7. Fix the pane in place with
   panel pins.

8. Work the putty into place
   with thumb, pushing firmly.

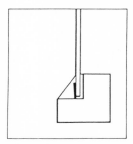

9. With a putty knife or sharp
   blade, angle the putty as
   shown.

10. When the putty is dry, paint
    the putty and the frame.

GATHERING INFORMATION

Step 1

a) Put these instructions in order:

   Angle the putty.
   Measure the frame.
   Take out all the old glass.
   Fix the pane with panel pins.
   Paint the putty and the frame.
   Remove the putty.
   Put the new pane into position.
   Take out the panel pins.
   Put the strip of putty round the inside of the frame.
   Put putty round the new pane.
   Buy the new pane.
   Clean the frame.

```
Step 6        Adverbs

Remove the broken glass carefully.

Put suitable adverbs in these sentences:

i)    Scrape away the old putty.
ii)   Clean the frame.
iii)  Measure the frame.
iv)   Fit the new pane.
v)    Put in the panel pins.
vi)   Work the putty into the frame.
vii)  Angle the putty.
viii) Paint the frame.
```

```
TASK

This is a picture of a metal frame window.  Make a set of instructions for
replacing the pane of glass.  (Note: metal frame windows can rust easily.)
```

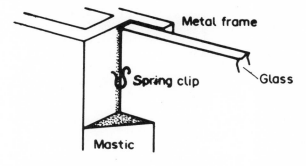

(*Hutchinson and Waters 1983: 103–9*)

▶ ## TASK 101

What criteria have been utilized in sequencing the activities?

Do the tasks increase in difficulty from the beginning to the end of the unit?

What factors seem to be involved in task difficulty?

The Hutchinson and Waters example is taken from the field of ESP. As with general purpose syllabuses, different ESP syllabuses will be located at different points along the product/process continuum.

The contents pages below and opposite have been taken from another ESP publication, *English in Focus: Biological Science*.

Contents

vi *Contents*

(Pearson 1979: v–vi)

▶ TASK 102

From the above sections of the contents page, do you think the coursebook will be either product-oriented or process-oriented? In other words, do you think the course is basically designed to develop students' knowledge of biological science or the skill of thinking and reasoning like a biological scientist? (You may decide that it is trying to do both.)

8.7 Teaching grammar as process

In Section One we looked briefly at the work of Rutherford, who argues for the inclusion of grammar as a central element in the curriculum. Here we shall look at applications of Rutherford's ideas. I am dealing with these here rather than in 7 because Rutherford is basically concerned with grammar as process rather than product. This is evident in the following:

> Given all that we presently know about language, how it is learned, and how it can be taught, the 'grammatical' part of a 'grammatical syllabus' does not entail specification of the language content at all; rather, it specifies how that language content (chosen in accordance with a variety of other, non-linguistic criteria) is to be exploited. The immediate reasons for not assigning a specifying role to grammar are worth reiterating. Grammatical specification in the syllabus has to result in the selection and ordering of grammatical constructs — a necessarily linear and sequential display of language items for learner input. Language acquisition, on the other hand, is not a linear progression, but a cyclic one, or even a metamorphic one. That is, the learner is constantly engaged in reanalysing data, reformulating hypotheses, recasting generalizations etc.
> (*Rutherford 1987: 159*)

The following tasks, which have been extracted from Rutherford's book, give some idea of how his ideas might be applied in practice.

A Which, if any, of these sentences contains an error? Find the errors and correct them.

> 1. In Lake Maracaibo was discovered the oil.
> 2. After a few minutes the guests arrived.
> 3. In my country does not appear to exist any constraint on women's rights. etc.

B Which is the most appropriate conversational response: Why?

> 1. A Is he leaving now?
>   B Yes, he is, because he has an appointment.
> 2. A Is he leaving now?
>   B Because he has an appointment.
> 3. A Why is he leaving now?
>   etc.

C Which of the following statements is implied by the text?

> The passing of the bill has given rise to further bitterness among the various linguistic communities in the province.
>
> 1. The various linguistic communities are bitter.
> 2. Bitterness caused the bill to be passed.
> 3. The province is bitter at the linguistic community.

D Select the appropriate words to complete the sentences.
(Note: This task has been completed by the author.)

Although the Province of Quebec has resisted efforts

to ~~avoid~~ ~~deny~~ deprive ~~forbid~~ ~~keep~~ ~~prevent~~ ~~prohibit~~ | it of its French-speaking identity no one can say that he is | ~~avoided~~ ~~denied~~ ~~deprived~~ forbidden ~~prevented~~ ~~prohibited~~

to speak English. That is, in making French the official language of Quebec, the laws still do not ~~avoid~~ ~~deny~~ ~~deprive~~ ~~forbid~~ keep prevent prohibit anyone

from speaking whatever language he chooses. Some people speak French and avoid ~~deny~~ ~~deprive~~ ~~forbid~~ ~~keep~~ ~~prevent~~ ~~prohibit~~ speaking English.

In Canada they don't ~~avoid~~ deny ~~deprive~~ ~~forbid~~ ~~keep~~ ~~prevent~~ ~~prohibit~~ you your rights.

(continued)

E Select the appropriate form of the sentence.

Weathering and erosion of rock exposed to the atmosphere constantly remove particles from the rock.

a	b	c
1. These rock particles are called sediment.	Sediment is what these rock particles are called.	What these rock particles are called is sediment.

a	b
2. The upper layers press down on the lower ones as sediments accumulate.	As sediments accumulate, the upper layers press down on the lower ones.

a	b
3. Sediments that stick together form sedimentary rocks.	Sedimentary rocks are formed by sediments that stick together.

a	b
4. Such rocks have been able to survive the test of time only in this way.	Only in this way have such rocks been able to survive the test of time.

F Show the relationship between the words in italics by drawing an arrow.

1. That was *a terrible thing to do.*

2. That was *a terrible thing to happen.*

G What do the italicized words refer to?

After *they* save a little money, Howard and Ellen wanted to buy a house. So they *did*. The floor plan was almost exactly the same as *that* of Ellen's parents' home, where *she* was reared. Buying *it* was not easy for *the young couple*, but Ellen was determined to go through with *it*. *She* could not stand living in their small apartment any longer. She wanted the kind of space *that* she had always lived with. Howard couldn't quite understand *his* wife's insistence on moving to more spacious quarters. *Their* small apartment was big enough for *him*. In fact *it* was almost like *the one* he had lived in as a child. But he could remember *his* mother saying almost daily, 'If only *I* had more room'.

H and I Rewrite the texts in normal English.

Dear Sir:
   I am writing in response to *your company's announcement* [AND *your company's announcement* appeared in last Sunday's edition of the Tampa Herald] of an opening for a systems analyst. [I assume that the position has not already been filled] I enclose *my résumé* [AND one more piece of information should now be added to *my résumé*]. etc.

> *The Norse explorer, Leif Ericson, succeeded in* _____
>
> The Norse
>
> _____, *but*
> explorer reaches the shores of Canada about 1000 A.D.
>
> *it is thought* _____
> The history of the white man there doesn't
>
> _____. *In 1497 John Cabot, in the service*
> begin until much later
>
> *of Henry VII, managed* _____
> John Cabot reaches the shores of Nova
>
> _____ . . . etc.
> Scotia

J   Complete the sentences in normal English.

> 1. Many French Canadians find [They learn English] important.
> 2. Quebec makes [Quebec preserves its French-speaking identity] a
>   rule.
> 3. Quebec takes [French is to be given priority over English] for
>   granted.
> 4. The government left [Will French be the official language of
>   Quebec?] up to the people to decide.

(*Rutherford 1987*)

▶   ## TASK 103

Bygate (1987:3) suggests that there is an important difference
between 'knowledge about a language and skill in using it'.

Do you think that Rutherford's tasks are trying to develop
knowledge about a language or skill in using it?

What do you think learners will gain from carrying out the tasks?

How useful do you think these activities are?

8.8 Conclusion

In 8 we have looked at some of the ways in which the theoretical aspects of
selecting and grading learning processes have been applied. We have seen
that the grading of learning tasks is particular complicated, and that
different syllabus designers and coursebook writers have looked to
different criteria in carrying out such tasks.

9 Selecting and grading objectives

9.1 Introduction

We shall now look at applications of the ideas presented in 5. In particular, we shall look at the distinctions between product-oriented and process-oriented objectives, and real-world and pedagogic objectives.

9.2 Product-oriented objectives

Product-oriented objectives describe the things that a learner will be able to do as a result of instruction. Product, or, as they are more usually called, performance objectives may be couched in different terms. For example, they may refer to grammatical, functional, thematic, or topical skills and knowledge.

The extract on the facing page has been taken from the Washington State Adult Refugee ESL Master Plan.

▶ TASK 104

Indicate the principal focus of each of these objectives.

Is the syllabus basically grammatical, functional, or topical in its orientation, or is it an attempt at developing an integrated syllabus?

Are the objectives all at the same level of difficulty, or are some more difficult than others?

If you were developing a teaching programme from this syllabus, what is the order in which you would teach these objectives? (That is, how would you grade the objectives?)

What criteria did you use in grading the objectives?

Preliterate I
Oral/Aural

The student is able to:

O/A 1   Make statements and ask questions related to personal and family information.

O/A 2   Exchange simple, common expressions of greeting and leave-taking.

O/A 3   Identify and state the names of cardinal numbers from 0–100.

O/A 4   Identify and state the names of the letters of the alphabet.

O/A 5   Follow one-step directions and commands (e.g., come in, put it down).

O/A 6   Ask and respond to questions about time.

O/A 7   Identify and count currency.

O/A 8   Make statements and ask questions about health problems and states of being (e.g., I'm tired. My _____ hurts).

O/A 9   Ask and respond to yes/no questions which verify family information, directions, time, money amounts, health problems, parts of the body, colors, sizes, and/or shapes.

O/A 10   Identify and name the basic colors (e.g., red, blue, yellow, green, orange, black, white).

O/A 11   Identify and name basic sizes (e.g., big, small).

O/A 12   Identify and name basic body parts.

O/A 13   Identify days of week in order.

O/A 14   Ask and respond to who, what, when, where, and how many requests.

O/A 15   Ask and respond to questions using common action verbs in the simple present and present continuous tenses (e.g., come, go, put, bring, buy, give, take, open, close).

O/A 16   Respond to questions about weather (e.g., rain, cold, snow).

O/A 17   Indicate lack of understanding or need for repetition (e.g., 'I don't understand,' 'Please repeat').

O/A 18   Identify and inquire about classroom objects.

O/A 19   Use personal pronouns and possessive pronouns and adjectives.

(*Callaway 1985: 23*)

The next extract is taken from the Hawaii English Program which was developed for teaching schoolchildren rather than adults.

Language skills

K-6 Language Skills: Non-graded, largely non-text, multi-media, self-instructional or peer-taught packages of materials to help the student toward progressively greater synthesized control of his language performance.

Instructional unit	*Objectives*	*Materials*

Listening-Speaking

The materials in this section are most often used in a two-part communication system consisting of a listener and a speaker. Although listening and speaking constitute one process, the speech communication process, the skills have been separated to make it possible for the learner to focus on one aspect of this process at a time.

Instructional unit	*Objectives*	*Materials*
1. Sounds of English (E)	The child discriminates between and produces English sounds that may be difficult for children.	35 audio-card booklets and 35 picture booklets, diagnostic audio cards and worksheets
2. Dialect Markers (DM)	The child discriminates between and produces English sounds that are often confused by Island children.	15 audio-card booklets and 15 picture booklets, diagnostic audio cards and worksheets
3. Intonation (Int)	The child discriminates between and produces statement and yes/no question intonation patterns.	6 sets of audio cards
4. Stress	The child discriminates between and produces contrasted stress patterns.	4 speaker, 4 listener booklets
5. Colors and Shapes (C&S)	The child recognizes and names 12 colors and 7 shapes.	3 sets audio cards, 3 sets flashcards, diagnostic worksheets
6. Prepositions (Prep)	The child recognizes and uses prepositions such as *on*, *under*, *through* and *around* appropriately.	9 sets audio cards, various manipulative materials (wooden block, wood cube, string), 4 laminated sheets

(*Hawaii English Program 1975: 1*)

► TASK 105

In what ways are these objectives similar to/different from those in the Washington State syllabus?

In what ways do both of these extracts reflect the target groups for which they were designed?

What assumptions by their authors about the nature of language and language learning are revealed in these extracts?

In 5 we saw that formal performance objectives are supposed to have three parts: a statement of what the learner is to do, under what conditions, and with what degree of skill. The difficulty level of the objectives is governed by the interaction between task, conditions, and standards.

In practice, many syllabuses focus on the specification of learner performance and either omit or detail separately the conditions and standards.

► TASK 106

Write (C) or (S) after each of the following to indicate whether they are conditions of standards.

1 the amount of repetition permitted
2 the degree of grammatical accuracy displayed
3 the source of the text — whether live or recorded, authentic or simulated
4 whether the interlocutor is or is not used to dealing with non-native speakers
5 whether performance is rehearsed or unrehearsed
6 the degree of fluency, intelligibility
7 the amount of assistance provided
8 the length/ size of utterances/ texts required
(*Adapted from Nunan 1985*)

Select five of the objectives from the Washington State syllabus and add standards and conditions to make them: (1) easier (2) more difficult.

It has been suggested that if the syllabus is to be more than a random collection of statements about learner performance, it is necessary for them to be linked to superordinate goals.

► TASK 107

The following objectives have been adapted from the Royal Society of Arts Certificate of English as a Second Language. Suggest a superordinate goal for them.

1 express own point of view in a group discussion
2 signal lack of understanding; ask for repetition and/or clarification
3 make arrangements involving time and location
4 give an account of an experience in logical, sequential, chronological order
5 give a description of an object, or person, related to an event or personal experience
6 ask or respond to a number of related questions in order to obtain or give advice or opinion
7 make appropriate apology and response
8 exchange greetings and personal details with sympathetic interlocutor

These could all be subsumed under a goal such as 'to provide learners with the language and skills necessary to participate in casual conversations'. Some of them could also appear under other goal statements. For instance, the objective: 'ask or respond to a number of related questions in order to obtain or give advice or opinion' could be subsumed under the goal, 'To obtain information for a specific purpose'. The following objectives have been extracted from the Washington State syllabus:

1 state and respond to common oral instructions used during the Washington State Driver's Examination
2 state and follow the steps in a complex process of five to seven steps (e.g. clean a household appliance, assemble a toy or a piece of equipment, set a multi-functional watch)
3 give information over the phone (e.g. job enquiries, directory assistance, working hours, appointment)
4 state and follow common medical and safety instructions (e.g. treatment plan, dosages, warning labels)
5 notify and state reasons for absence from work or school for self and child
6 give and respond to warnings (e.g. 'Watch out!' 'Don't touch!' 'Stop!')
7 identify, state and/or follow on-the-job rules and school regulations
8 make statements and ask questions using common action verbs and 'be' and 'do' in simple present and present continuous tenses

▶ TASK 108

In 5, it was pointed out that objectives could be couched in terms of real-world performance, or in terms of activities which learners are to carry out in the classroom.

Which of the objectives in the above list refer to:

1 real-world tasks, i.e. tasks which the learner could conceivably be required to carry out in the real world?

2 classroom tasks, i.e. tasks which it would be highly unlikely for the learner.to carry out outside the language classroom, but which are thought to facilitate learning?

3 both real-world and classroom tasks?

Which, if any, of the above real-world objectives would it not be practical to teach in class?

Can you think of pedagogic objectives which might be written to facilitate the acquisition of real-world skills?

► TASK 109

The following objectives are not the sort of things individuals are likely to be required to do outside the classroom. Can you think of any reasons why they might, nonetheless, be useful objectives to have in a language course?

1 In a classroom role play, ask and answer questions relating to personal details. Responses to be comprehensible to someone unused to dealing with non-English speakers.

2 Read the following newspaper article and identify the antecedents of the underlined anaphoric reference items. Eight of the ten items to be correctly identified.

3 Listen to a taped radio news bulletin and identify the news headlines. Four of the six headlines to be correctly identified.

4 Indicate, by placing a circle around the correct alternative, which items in a vocabulary list occur as key words in a news broadcast.

5 Indicate ability to follow a narrative by listening to a story and placing a series of pictures in the correct sequence.

6 Demonstrate the ability to decode regular sound/symbol relationships in school texts.

7 Sight-read key function words when they occur in context.

8 Extract relevant information from a recorded dialogue and complete a table.

Coursebooks do not always explicitly state what it is the learner should be able to do as a result of undertaking a particular activity or unit of work. However, it should be possible to rewrite coursebook content in the form of objectives (i.e. in a form which states what learners will do in and out of class).

► TASK 110

Study the following activity from *The Cambridge English Course* and write at least one objective which learners should be able to perform as a result of completing the activity.

Unit 10

Appearances

A Sheila has got long dark hair

1 **Put the right names with the pictures.**

Sheila has got long dark hair and brown eyes.
Helen has got long red hair and green eyes.
Mary has got long fair hair and green eyes.
Lucy has got short grey hair and blue eyes.

2 Ask the teacher questions.

What's this?

It's your mouth.

What are these?

Ears.

3 Test other students. Do they know these words?

hair   eyes   nose   ears   mouth   face
arm   hand   foot   leg

TOUCH YOUR RIGHT EYE.

TOUCH YOUR LEFT EAR.

4 Talk about yourself and other people. Examples:

'I've got small hands. My mother has got pretty hair.'

5 Write three sentences with *and*, and three with *but*. Examples:

I've got blue eyes, and my mother has, too. I've got straight hair, but my brother's got curly hair.

6 Listening for information. Listen to the recording and fill in the table.

	height	hair colour	face	eyes	good-looking?
Steve's wife	5ft 8				*don't know*
Lorna's mum			*pale*		
Ruth's friend					
Katy's son					
Sue's husband					

(*Swan and Walter 1984: 42*)

► ## TASK 111

What is your opinion on the relationship between syllabuses and coursebooks?

Do you think that in the case of comprehensive coursebooks such as *The Cambridge English Course* 'syllabus' and 'coursebook' are synonymous?

In some educational systems, teachers are provided with course outlines consisting of frames which they can use, adapt, or modify in developing their courses. The syllabus frame which follows overleaf has been taken from Wylie and Sunderland (1982). It is intended to help teachers working with adult immigrants.

► ## TASK 112

Study the learning objectives set out in the frame overleaf.

How appropriate are these objectives for the content which is specified?

Are the objectives designed for beginning, intermediate, or advanced students?

What conditions and standards might be added to the objectives to turn them into three-part performance objectives?

► ## TASK 113

As we saw in 5, one criticism of product-oriented objectives is that they frequently fail to indicate how the objective is to be achieved.

Refer back to the extract from Clark and Hamilton (1984:30) preceding Task 84.

The syllabus guidelines from which this extract was taken attempt to provide a link between objectives and tasks.

Write out three performance objectives based on the extract, to include performance, conditions, and standards.

FUNCTION	NOTIONS	POSSIBLE CONTEXTS	CULTURAL CONTENT	SKILLS & ACTIVITIES
1 GREETINGS AND GOODBYES a) Greeting b) Asking how the other person is c) Telling how one is d) Saying goodbye e) Inviting someone to come in f) Inviting someone to sit down g) Thanking	GREETING FAREWELL POLITENESS (UN)FAMILIARITY PRESENT TIME POINT OF TIME SOCIAL CONVENTION RECIPROCITY GRATITUDE	.classroom with teacher, other students, visitors .child-care centre .children's school with teacher, other parents .local shop .in the street .social gathering .doctor's, dentist's surgery .workplace .over the fence .postcard .letter .note (to teacher)	.gesture for *sit down* .beckoning normally with palm up; crooked index finger not obscene .waving as greeting (distant) and goodbye .frequently simultaneous reciprocation of greeting, goodbye, and inquiry .use of *thank you* (for the thought/invitation) (See also CULTURAL CONTENT Group 7) .when a list of ailments can be an appropriate response to *How are you?* .norms of physical contact (same and opposite sex) in public e.g. kissing, males walking with arms around each other .the Australian weekend .conventions of opening and closing letters	.number bingo

EXAMPLES	LEARNING OBJECTIVES

Hello, how are you (today)?
Good, thanks. How are you?
Fine, thank you.
 	
Come in.
 	
Sit down.
Thank you.
 	
See you on Monday.
See you.
Bye.
 	
Dear Miss Robinson,
            Yours sincerely
 	
See you at 11.
 	
Dear Jill,
      ......
 	
Dear Sir
 	
Have a good weekend.
Thanks, same to you.
 	
Excuse me, I must go now.
 	
Good morning.
 	
Hi!
	.use* greetings and goodbyes in EXAMPLES column, plus other appropriate phrases e.g. *goodnight, Dear Sir/Madam* (See RATIONALE – Distribution and Recycling p.19 and Consolidation p.26)
	.use *come in, sit down*
	.use names of days of the week
	.use numbers to 60 in spoken form (NB *fifteen* versus *fifty*)
	.use numerals to 60 in written form (NB 1 and 7)
	.use time of day, first as in digital – *eleven fifteen*
	.use time phrases – *today, this afternoon, tonight, tomorrow, at 1 o'clock, at midday,* etc. (NB unstressed syllables)
	.recognise alternative way(s) of inviting someone to sit down, e.g. *Take a seat*
	.use wave as distant greeting and as goodbye
	.recognise non-verbal support for inviting someone to come in and sit down and respond appropriately
	
	*To 'use' a phrase means to recognise its total meaning and to respond appropriately, and produce it where appropriate. To 'recognise' means to respond appropriately to the total meaning of a phrase but not to produce it.

(Wylie and Sunderland 1982)

9.3 Process-oriented objectives

Process objectives focus, not on the outcomes of instruction, but on the classroom activities themselves. The extract from Clark and Hamilton referred to in Task 113 can be seen as an attempt to reconcile both process and product objectives.

▶ TASK 114

How successful is this attempted reconciliation?

How important is it for syllabus designers to specify both the means and the ends of instruction?

The following extract is from Clark and Hamilton (1984).

Stages one and two

Event	*Possible Functional Content*	*Possible Notional Content*
D3.1 Seeking information through conversation	Politeness Attracting attention Seeking information Reacting to information Seeking clarification Thanking	Whether there is and how to get to: (availability, existence and direction) a) Station, underground station, bus stop, ferry c) Café, restaurant d) Hotel, campsite, toilet e) Various shops and markets related to food and drink, clothes, toiletries, medicines, postcards, writing materials, souvenirs, gifts, films for photography, newspapers, magazines, books, records, camping needs, etc. f) Post office, police station, cinema, swimming pool. Sights in general, i.e. castle, monument, zoo etc.

(continued)

D3.2 Buying through face to face conversation	Politeness Reacting to request to help Asking for things Expressing wish for something	e) Goods – see suggested list above f) Stamps at post office
	Giving information about intended purchases Seeking information Asking for suggestions or advice/reacting appropriately Asking for/giving Reacting to comment Transacting payment Thanking	Quantity, size, colour, style Availability, price Best buy for a particular purpose Approval, disapproval, suitability, too expensive, too big/small, etc. Money, change

(*Clark and Hamilton 1984:41*)

► ## TASK 115

Select one of the six events presented by Clark and Hamilton and write out:

1 product objectives
2 corresponding process objectives.

Do you think that specifying both product and process adds anything of value to the tasks? If so, what?

In Task 68, you were asked to decide whether there was any real distinction between real-world, product, pedagogic, and process objectives. Review the decision you came to and decide whether, having looked at a variety of objectives, you would like to change your mind.

► ## TASK 116

Review the process objectives you have written and decide on how these might be graded.

To what extent do your grading criteria reflect those established for grading tasks and activities in 8?

Would it be appropriate to add conditions and/or standards to process objectives?

Do you think that the notion of adding standards is inconsistent with the notion of process objectives?

9.4 Conclusion

In 9 we have studied examples of different types of objectives. We have seen that some objectives relate to real-world tasks, while others relate to classroom tasks. Some objectives can be related to superordinate goal statements, while for others this is more difficult. A distinction is drawn between product-oriented and process-oriented objectives. Difficulty levels, and therefore grading criteria for product-oriented goals, can be found in the specification of conditions and standards. Establishing levels of difficulty for process objectives is much more difficult, although work being carried out by people such as Anderson and Lynch (1988) should, in the future, help us in setting grading criteria.

Exploring syllabus design

10 General principles

10.1 Curriculum and syllabus models

Not all of the following tasks will be relevant for all readers. Only attempt those tasks which are relevant and useful to you in your own particular teaching situation.

Where one task presupposes the completion of a preceding task, or utilizes resources from it, this will be indicated.

▶ TASK 117

Aim
To criticize the curriculum model operating in your own teaching system.

Resources
Curriculum documents, statements, and outlines from your teaching institution.

Sample curriculum models such as those presented in **1**.

Procedure
Study the curriculum documents you have collected.

Using these, and your own introspection, draw a diagram to represent the curriculum model operating in the system in which you work.

Evaluation
Are there any notable omissions from the model? Is its major point of focus on planning, implementation, or assessment?

Which of the following elements are included or excluded from consideration in the curriculum documents?

- needs analysis
- goals and objectives
- content specification
- learning tasks and activities
- resources and materials
- curriculum implementation
- curriculum management
- learner assessment
- programme evaluation
- teacher development

Which of these is the major point of focus in the curriculum?

► # TASK 118

Aim
To identify some of the assumptions underlying the language curriculum of your institution.

Resources
As for Task 117.

Procedure
Study the documents and make brief notes on the following:
– beliefs about language, teaching, and learning incorporated into the documents
– assumptions about learners' needs
– assumptions about the context in which learning occurs

Make a list of the questions you would like to put to the author(s) of the documents you have studied.

Evaluation
To what extent do you agree or disagree with the assumptions underlying the curriculum on which your language programmes are based?

Can you think of any strategies to change, modify, or adapt aspects of the curriculum with which you disagree?

How would you answer the questions you have set for the curriculum planners?

► # TASK 119

Aim
To compare the idealized view of the curriculum with what actually happens in reality.

Resources
As for Tasks 117 and 118.

Procedure
Compare the idealized view of the curriculum, as set out in the curriculum documents, with the reality as you know it, i.e. the 'real' curriculum which is enacted in classrooms each day.

Make a list of all the things which, in your view, distinguish the idealized curriculum from the enacted curriculum.

Evaluation
How great is the gap between the ideal and the reality?

To what extent would it be desirable or feasible to try and close this gap?

Which, in your opinion, should be modified, the ideal or the reality?

Is the gap between the ideal and the reality due largely to educational, administrative, financial, or political factors?

▶ TASK 120

Aim
To identify the scope of the syllabus(es) you are currently using.

Resources
The set of statements on syllabus design extracted from Brumfit (1984) and reproduced in **1.3**.

Sets of syllabus statements and outlines.

Procedure
Study the syllabus statements and outlines which form the basis for your programme planning and make a list of those elements which are included in the syllabus.

Compare this list with the set of statements in **1.3** on syllabus design.

Extract those statements which reflect the view of syllabus underlying your syllabus outlines and documents.

Using one or more of the statements from Brumfit as a guide, write a definition of syllabus which is consistent with the syllabus statements and outlines.

Evaluation
What are the similarities and differences between your own syllabus statement and those in Brumfit?

Does your statement represent a broad or narrow view?

▶ TASK 121

Aim
To identify those areas of the syllabus amenable to modification or adaptation by the teacher.

Resources
Syllabus documents, programming procedures, and statements from your own teaching institution.

Procedure
Analyse your own teaching situation and write down those areas of the syllabus in which teacher intervention might be possible.

Make a list of the strategies which could be employed to facilitate teacher intervention.

Evaluation
To what extent is it feasible for teachers to modify or adapt the syllabus you are using?

► # TASK 122

Aim
To compare the syllabus you are using with that used in a similar institution.

Resources
Syllabus documents, programming procedures, and statements from your own and a comparable institution.

Procedure
Analyse and compare the two sets of documents.

Evaluation
What are the similarities and differences between the two?

Do the documents reveal discernible differences in beliefs about the nature of language and language learning?

What are these?

10.2 Purposes and goals

► # TASK 123

Aim
To evaluate the use of biographical information in syllabus planning and adaptation.

Resources
A biographical data collection form.

Procedure
Develop a biographical data collection form. This may be adapted from the sample form that precedes Task 13 in **2.3**. At this stage, restrict your focus to biographical data, e.g. age, years of formal education, nationality, and first language, current proficiency level, length of time in target culture, number and duration of previous language courses, present and intended occupation, and other language(s) spoken. (Needless to say, not all this information will be relevant or applicable to the students you teach. Develop a form to reflect your own situation.)

Interview a sample of students from your own classes and those of your colleagues.

Review the data you have collected.

Evaluation
What are the similarities and differences between students?

Do the data provide any useful information on how learners might most effectively be grouped?

How useful did you find the data collecting exercise from a syllabus planning perspective?

▶ TASK 124

Aim
To evaluate the use of instructional analysis in syllabus planning.

Resources
The following needs analysis form:

Participant
Purposive domain
Setting
Interaction
Instrumentality
Dialect
Communicative event
Communicative key

Procedure
Complete the needs analysis form for a group of students you are currently teaching, or for a group you have previously taught.

List the ways in which this information might be used for writing or modifying a syllabus for the students in question.

Evaluation
Which categories did you find relatively easy to complete?

Which did you find difficult?

Which information do you think is useful to collect for syllabus planning purposes?

Which do you think is not very useful or relevant?

▶ TASK 125

Aim
To evaluate the subjective needs and preferences of your students.

Resources
The learning preference survey form related to Task 73.

Procedure
Study the form and modify it by deleting items which are obviously inappropriate for your students or teaching situation.

Survey each student in one of your classes and the class of a colleague by asking students to respond to each of the statements according to the key that accompanies the form.

Total the responses for each statement and then rank these from highest to lowest.

Evaluation

Did this task provide you with information which could be useful to you in adopting or adapting a syllabus for the learners who were surveyed?

What are some of the ways the useful information might be used in syllabus design?

Do these learners seem to favour (1) a traditional (2) a communicative, or (3) an eclectic or 'mixed' approach to instruction?

What similarities or differences are there between the two groups of students?

Are there any students whose responses are seriously at odds with those of their peers?

Were you surprised by any of the results you obtained?

Were there any mismatches between the preferences of your students and your own preferences?

▶ TASK 126

Aim
To compare preferences of different teachers.

Resources
A copy of the survey form you used in the above task, modified so that it is applicable to teachers (e.g. item 1 might now read 'I like to get my students to practice sounds and pronunciation').

Procedure
Get the language teachers (or a sample of teachers) to complete the form.

If you think it desirable, share the results you obtain with your colleagues, and note their reactions.

Evaluation
What similarities or differences are there between the responses provided by the teachers?

How do you account for these similarities or differences?

Were you surprised by any of the responses?

What did you learn about your colleagues from this task?

Did you share the results with your colleagues?

If so, what were their reactions?

Did any of your colleagues indicate that they might modify their practices or beliefs as a result of the exercise?

▶ # TASK 127

Aim
To explore the possibility of developing more flexible grouping arrangements.

Resources
A survey form such as the one used in Task 125, or one adapted from those presented in Sections One and Two.

Procedure
Administer the survey to a range of students in your own and colleagues' classes.

Analyse the results and see whether the learners might be subdivided for parts of the teaching day according to their responses to the survey.

Discuss the results with your colleagues.

Evaluation
How feasible would it be, in your institution, to subgroup learners according to their preferences, needs, and interests for different parts of the teaching day?

What would be the likely impediments to such an experiment?
Are these chiefly pedagogical, ideological, or administrative?

▶ # TASK 128

Aim
To explore the relationship between syllabus goals and the goals of language teachers.

Resources
Syllabus outlines, documents, and statements from your teaching institution.

The language goal survey form overleaf.

Procedure
Study the syllabus outlines, documents, and statements from your institution, and assign a number from 1 (low) to 5 (high) to each of the goal statements on the form according to their perceived prominence in the syllabus documents.

Ask the teachers in your institution to indicate the importance of the goal statements by rating each from 1 to 5.

Evaluation
Are there any mismatches between the teachers' ratings and those you derived from the syllabus documents?

If there are mismatches, can you think of any ways in which these might be resolved?

Our language program has been designed to achieve the following goals:

1 to contribute to the intellectual, personal, and vocational development of the individual

2 to acquire the competence to use English in real-life situations for the development and maintenance of interpersonal relationships, and to take part in interpersonal encounters through the sharing of factual and attitudinal information

3 to develop and maintain a sense of confidence and self-worth

4 to develop the skills needed to acquire, record, and use information from a variety of aural and written sources

5 to develop mastery over English as a written system and to have some knowledge of how it works at the levels of phonology, morphology, and syntax

6 to increase, through a common language, the possibility of understanding, friendship, and co-operation with people who speak English

7 to foster the development of critical thinking skills, and skills in 'learning how to learn'

8 to develop the skills and attitudes to use English for creative and imaginative purposes

9 to develop the English needed to get a job requiring the use of English

10.3 Syllabus products

▶   TASK 129

Aim
To examine the selection and sequencing of grammatical elements in a syllabus you are currently using.

Resources
A detailed syllabus outline or list of contents from a coursebook you are currently using for beginning students.

The list of contents (opposite) from *Contemporary English, Book 1.*

Procedure
Compare the list of contents with the syllabus outline or coursebook you are currently using.

Evaluation
What are the similarities and differences between the two sets of contents?

How would you account for these?

Are there any notable omissions in your own syllabus? What are these?

Is the sequencing appropriate? If not, could any of the items be re-sequenced?

Unit	Verb Phrase	Noun Phrase	Prepositional Phrase	Sentence	
ONE	is; isn't (is not)	a; an; the; it that; this singular nouns numerals	on; in; near; of	What...? Where...? Is...?	1
TWO	are; aren't	they plurals		Are...? and	7
THREE	can (permission)	very adjectives (colours) (nationality words) he; she article+profession	with; from	be+N+adj? How old...? What colour...? Who...?	13
FIRST REVIEW AND COMPLEMENTATION UNIT I; you; we; these; those					19
FOUR	am	her; his; my; your (poss. adj.) I; you (months)	under	so What...like?	23
FIVE	present progressive	her; him; them; us postmodification with prep. phrase	to at (the moment)	What...doing?	29
SIX	can; can't (ability)	the time	past; to	What time...? How? but	35
SECOND REVIEW AND COMPLEMENTATION UNIT our; their; possessive pronouns					41
SEVEN	Present Simple (3rd person singular)		at (time) by (transport)	then Does...?	45
EIGHT	Present Simple (other persons)			Do...? How much...? (price)	51
NINE	has; have never once/twice a week, etc.	no (as det.) each		How much...? (quantity) How many...? How often...?	57
TEN	stative verbs present simple with frequency words	another other	on (day) in (part of day) in (season) after; before		63

(Rossner, Shaw, Shepherd, Taylor, and Davies 1979)

▶ TASK 130

Aim
To critique the selection and presentation of grammatical items in a coursebook you are currently using.

Resources
A coursebook you are currently using or have recently used.

Procedure
Study the selection and presentation of grammatical items from a representative selection of units or chapters in the coursebook.

Evaluation
How are the grammatical items introduced?

Is there adequate contextualization for the items? (Are they presented and practised within a meaningful or communicative context?)

▶ TASK 131

Aim
To examine the integration of grammatical, functional, and notional components in a syllabus you are currently using.

Resources
A detailed syllabus outline or coursebook you are currently using or have recently used which incorporates grammatical, functional, and notional elements.

Procedure
Extract from the syllabus outline or coursebook a list of the grammatical, functional, and/or notional elements which are covered.

Compare these lists and note the ways in which the elements are related and integrated.

Evaluation
How are the elements related?

Are the relationships arbitrary or not?

How well are the elements interrelated from your own perspective?

If there are any elements which are not related in a satisfactory or convincing way, can you think of ways in which this could be improved?

▶ TASK 132

Aim
To compare grammatical sequences in your syllabus with those proposed by SLA researchers.

Resources
A syllabus outline containing graded grammatical structures. The following table showing stages of acquisition for selected grammatical items.

Stage	Item	Example
2	SVO word order	I like Chinese food. I can swim.
3	Adverbs in initial/final position *Yes/no* questions with *do*	Now, I must go. Do you like this?
4	*Yes/no* questions with inversion *To* infinitive	Have you a car? I want to go.
5	3rd person singular *Wh-* questions with *do*	He works in a factory. Where do you work?
6	Question tags Adverbs in sentence internal position	He's German, isn't he? I can always go.

Table 5

Procedure
Compare the sequence of items in your syllabus with that suggested by research into speech-processing constraints.

Evaluation
What similarities and differences are there?

Provide a justification for the ordering of items in your syllabus (assuming that it differs from the order set out in the above table).

Given the context in which you are teaching, would it be possible or desirable to modify your syllabus in the light of currently available data from SLA research?

10.4 Experiential content

You will recall that experiential content refers to the topics, themes, situations, settings, and so on which provide a context for the linguistic content. The selection of experiential content is one task where there is potential for negotiation between learners and teachers.

► TASK 133

Aim
To explore the possibility of basing the selection of content on the interests of the learners.

Resources
A content survey form.

Procedure
Construct a content survey form (see overleaf) containing a range of topics of interest and relevance to your students, for which you have resources, and which you are prepared to teach.

> Indicate which of the following topics you would like to study by placing a circle around the appropriate number. (1 = 'I would not like to study this topic at all'; 5 = 'I would like to study this topic very much'.)
>
> | | | |
> |---|---|---|
> | 1 | Summer holidays in England | 1 2 3 4 5 |
> | 2 | Wedding invitations | 1 2 3 4 5 |
> | 3 | Bob Dylan | 1 2 3 4 5 |
> | 5 | Bus and train timetables | 1 2 3 4 5 |
> | 6 | Describing a house | 1 2 3 4 5 |
> | 7 | Camera-operating instructions | 1 2 3 4 5 |
> | 8 | The Olympic Games | 1 2 3 4 5 |
> | 9 | Stamp-dispensing machines | 1 2 3 4 5 |
> | 10 | Ernest Hemingway | 1 2 3 4 5 |
> | 11 | Recipe – making hamburgers | 1 2 3 4 5 |
> | 12 | Apollo moon landing | 1 2 3 4 5 |
> | 13 | Cassette player – how to use | 1 2 3 4 5 |
> | 14 | Comparing cars | 1 2 3 4 5 |
> | 15 | Job advertisements | 1 2 3 4 5 |
> | 16 | Motorcycles | 1 2 3 4 5 |
> | 17 | Road accident report | 1 2 3 4 5 |
> | 18 | The story of tea | 1 2 3 4 5 |

Administer the survey to your students, total the results, and rank the topics from most to least popular.

Discuss the results with your students.

Evaluation

What sort of consensus was there among the students?

Were you surprised by any of the results?

In what ways might you use the information you obtained to modify the syllabus you are currently using?

▶ # TASK 134

Aim

To explore the problem of grading experiential content.

Resources

The survey form and results of the activity in Task 133.

Procedure

It is not immediately apparent how topics such as those listed in the sample survey form can be graded.

Make a list of those criteria which could be used to grade and sequence the experiential content.

Evaluation

Which criteria might most usefully be used to grade content in your own situation?

Is it possible to develop thematic links between some of the items and use these to sequence the items?

10.5 Tasks and activities

▶ **TASK 135**

Aim

To examine the extent to which the syllabuses you use incorporate procedural elements.

Resources

The syllabus documents and outlines used in **10.1**.

Procedure

Study the syllabus outlines used in your institution and complete the following table by ranking the elements from 1 (most prominent) to 7 (least prominent) according to your perceptions of their importance in the syllabus.

Element	Rank
Real-world learning goals Grammatical items Functions Notions Situations Topics and themes Learning tasks and activities	

Table 6

Evaluation

What proportion of the syllabus is devoted to processes, and what to products?

In your opinion, is there a lack of balance in the syllabus documents?

If so, can you think of any ways in which this might be redressed? List these options.

Which of the options you have listed could be effected by you, the classroom teacher, and which require the involvement of others?

▶ **TASK 136**

Aim

To explore the distinction between real-world and pedagogic tasks and activities.

Resources
A sample list of tasks, either from a syllabus you are currently following or a coursebook.

Procedure
Following the distinction made in **4.3** between real-world and pedagogic tasks, divide the sample list of tasks from your syllabus or coursebook into those which the learner might be called upon in real life to perform, those which would not be performed in real life, and those which cannot be assigned to either group.

Evaluation
Is the syllabus or coursebook basically oriented towards the teaching of real-world or pedagogic tasks, or is there a balance between the two? What justification is or might be offered for the inclusion of the pedagogic tasks?

Were there any tasks you found difficult to assign to one or other category? If so, why?

What insights, if any, did this task give you into the assumptions about language and learning underlying your own syllabus?

▶ ## TASK 137

Aim
To apply the task-based procedure used here to your own situation.

Resources
The list of tasks used in Task 136.

Procedure
Following the procedure used in this section, write up each of the tasks you have selected in terms of 'Aim', 'Resources', 'Procedure', and 'Evaluation'.

Evaluation
Did you have any difficulties with any of the tasks? If so, what were they? What caused the problems?

Did you find that it was more difficult to formulate an aim than listing resources and describing procedure? If so, why do you think this was so?

Did you find this a useful exercise? Why or why not?

What insights, if any, did it provide you into the nature of the syllabuses or coursebooks you are using?

▶ ## TASK 138

Aim
To apply criteria for judging the worth of tasks to your own situation.

Resources
The list of tasks used in Tasks 136 and 137.

The following table adapted from Candlin (1986):

Criteria	Rating
1 promote attention to meaning, purpose, negotiation 2 encourage attention to relevant data 3 draw objectives from the communicative needs of learners 4 allow for flexible approaches to the task 5 allow for different solutions depending on skills/resources of learners 6 involve learner contributions, attitudes, and affects 7 are challenging but not threatening 8 require input from all learners 9 define a problem to be worked on by learners 10 involve language use in solving task 11 allow co-evaluation by learners and teachers 12 develop capacities to estimate consequences 13 provide opportunities for metacommunication 14 provide opportunities for language practice 15 promote training for problem-sensing and problem-solving 16 promote sharing of information and expertise 17 provide monitoring and feedback 18 heighten learners' consciousness and reflection 19 promote critical awareness about data and about language learning 20 offer a high return on investment and are cost-effective	

Table 7

Procedure
Select a representative sample of tasks. Provide a rating from 1 (low) to 5 (high) for each of the above criteria according to how well they represent the tasks you have selected.

Evaluation
What did this exercise tell you (1) about the learning tasks you examined (2) the criteria for judging the worth of tasks?

How might you utilize this information in syllabus modification and improvement?

▶ TASK 139

Aim
To apply criteria for judging the worth of tasks to your own situation.

Resources
The list of tasks used in Tasks 136, 137, and 138.

The following table adapted from Raths (1971):

Criteria	Rating
1 permit learners to make informed choices and reflect on consequences of their choice 2 assign active rather than passive roles to students 3 ask students to engage in inquiry into ideas, applications of intellectual processes, or current problems 4 involve learners with realia 5 completion may be accomplished at different levels of ability 6 ask students to apply existing skills or knowledge to a new setting 7 require students to examine topics or issues typically ignored 8 involve risk of success or failure 9 require students to rewrite, rehearse, polish initial efforts 10 involve students in application and mastery of meaningful rules, standards, or disciplines 11 give students a chance to share planning, carrying out of a plan, or results of an activity with others 12 relevant to expressed purposes of students	

Table 8

Procedure
Select a representative sample of tasks. Provide a rating from 1 (low) to 5 (high) for each of the above criteria according to how well they represent the tasks you have selected.

Evaluation
What did this exercise tell you (1) about the learning tasks you examined (2) the criteria for judging the worth of tasks?

How might you utilize this information in syllabus modification and improvement?

Were these criteria more or less useful in judging the worth of tasks than the set of criteria provided by Candlin?

Can you identify why one set of criteria was more useful than the other?

▶ TASK 140

Aim
To determine the criteria used for grading tasks in a syllabus or coursebook you are currently using.

Resources
A selection of tasks from a syllabus or coursebook.

Procedure
Study the tasks and, with reference to the material provided in **4** and **8**, list

those factors which seem to have been used by the syllabus designer/ coursebook writer in grading the tasks.

Rank these factors from most to least significant.

Evaluation
Are the factors used in grading the tasks basically linguistic, non-linguistic, or a combination of the two?

Could the order in which the tasks are presented be changed or not? Would it be (1) possible (2) desirable to modify the order? Why, or why not?

What inferences can you derive from the ways in which the items are presented about the attitude of the syllabus designer/coursebook writer to the classroom teacher (e.g. is there any evidence from the way the activities are presented and graded that the syllabus is meant to be 'teacher-proof')?

▶ ## TASK 141

Aim
To apply Widdowson's concepts of 'rehearsal' and 'investment' to your own syllabus.

Resources
As for Task 140.

Procedure
Examine a representative selection of tasks from your syllabus or coursebook in the light of Widdowson's distinction between 'rehearsal' and 'investment' type tasks (refer to **4.6**).

Evaluation
What percentage of tasks are aimed at 'investment' and what percentage at 'rehearsal'?

What, if anything, does this reveal about the attitudes of the syllabus designer/ coursebook writer on the nature of language and learning?

Is the balance of investment and rehearsal type tasks consistent with the goals of the syllabus, or are there inconsistencies? What are these?

Are there any ways in which any inconsistencies or imbalances could be redressed?

Do you think that Widdowson's distinction is a useful one?

10.6 Objectives

In this section, we shall apply some of the ideas developed and presented in 5 and 9.

▶ TASK 142

Aim
To explore the reformulation of syllabus content as objectives.

Resources
Syllabus outlines.
The following table:

Focus	Example
Grammatical	Learners will use present perfect appropriately in contrast with the simple past. Your examples:
Functional	Learners will make polite requests. Your examples:
Notional	Learners will express causality. Your examples:
Topical	Students will enquire about train departure times to specified destinations. Your examples:
Macroskill	Students will underline the main point in a written passage. Your examples:

Table 9

Procedure
Study the content specifications in your syllabus. Find examples of grammatical, functional, notional, topical, and macroskill content and express these in the form of objectives. (We have already seen that complete objectives consist of three parts: tasks, conditions, and standards. For this activity, focus only on the task element.)

Insert your examples at the relevant points in the above table.

Evaluation
How useful do you imagine it might be to have the syllabus content formulated in terms of what learners are able to do?

Do you think the objectives are of any value if they are formulated solely in terms of task, or do you think conditions and standards should also be added?

Is the emphasis in your syllabus on grammatical, functional, notional, or macroskill objectives?

Are there other content areas which have not been included in the above table (e.g. content which has a cognitive, cultural, or learning-how-to-learn focus)? What are they?

▶ TASK 143

(For syllabuses specified in terms of objectives)

Aim
To identify the type of objectives specified in your syllabus.

Resources
Sets of objectives from your syllabus.

Sample objectives from other sources such as those provided in 9.

Procedure
Compare the objectives in your syllabus with those provided in 9.

Note whether the objectives in your syllabus specify what learners should be able to do in the real world, in the classroom, or in both contexts.

If both, estimate the relative balance between the two types.

Evaluation
Is this balance a reasonable one, given the overall aims or goals of your syllabus?

If not, is there any way in which the imbalance might be redressed?

▶ TASK 144

Aim
To explore the relationship between tasks, conditions, and standards.

Resources
As for Task 143.

Procedure
Note whether your objectives contain conditions and standards.

If they do, decide whether these are appropriate (1) to the tasks (2) to the learners.

If they do not, insert conditions and standards into the statements of objectives.

Evaluation
Is it possible to write blanket statements of conditions and standards which might apply to a cluster of tasks, or are the conditions and standards peculiar to each task?

How useful and/or important do you think it is to specify conditions and standards? (Refer to your response in Task 142.)

▶ # TASK 145

Aim
To identify those factors which might affect the difficulty level of an objective.

Resources
Sets of objectives from your syllabus outlines or coursebooks. (If the content has been specified in terms of objectives, use these, otherwise use objectives you have developed in preceding tasks.)

Procedure
Study the objectives in detail, and make a list of those factors which might affect the difficulty level of the objectives.

Compare your list with the one below.

Factors affecting the difficulty of an objective
1 complexity of the language to which the learner is exposed
2 grammatical complexity of the language
3 speed at which the language is spoken
4 'authenticity' or otherwise of the text
5 amount of visual and non-verbal support provided
6 length of response demanded of the learner
7 number of speakers on the tape
8 degree of intelligibility demanded of the learner
9 familiarity of the subject matter
10 amount of stress placed upon the learner
11 complexity of the objective in terms of the number of steps involved
12 relevance of the objective to the learner

Evaluation
What are the similarities/ differences between the lists?

Which factors seem most prominent in determining the difficulty of objectives?

Which of those relate to conditions and which to standards?

What are the similarities and differences between these lists and the factors you listed for determining task difficulty in Task 58?

What does this tell you about 'task-based' and 'objectives-based' syllabuses? Do you think there is a difference between these two syllabus types or not? If so, what are they?

▶ # TASK 146

Aim
To explore the grading and sequencing of objectives.

Resources
As for Task 145.

Procedure
List the objectives in the order in which they might be taught.

Evaluation
Which factors were most important to you in determining the sequencing of the objectives?

Were there factors other than difficulty which influenced you in your grading? If so, what were these?

Glossary

analytic syllabus: a syllabus based on non-linguistic units such as topics, themes, settings, and situations. Learners are exposed to holistic 'chunks' of language and are required to extract patterns and regularities from these.

communicative approaches: approaches to language teaching in which the focus is on processes of communication rather than on structural, functional, or notional items.

curriculum: principles and procedures for the planning, implementation, evaluation, and management of an educational programme. Curriculum study embraces syllabus design (the selection and grading of content) and methodology (the selection of learning tasks and activities).

function: the communicative use to which an utterance or longer piece of language is put. Examples of functions include: apologizing, greeting, describing, defining, contradicting.

goal: the broad, general purposes behind a course of study. Goals can be couched in terms of what the teacher is to do or what the learner is to do. Examples of goals:
'To develop conversational skills.'
'To develop skills in learning-how-to-learn.'
'To teach learners basic grammatical structure.'
'To prepare learners for tertiary study in a foreign language.'

grading: the arrangement of syllabus content from easy to difficult.

methodology: the study and development of learning tasks and activities.

needs analysis: techniques and procedures for obtaining information from and about learners to be used in curriculum development.

notion: the concepts expressed through language. Examples of notions include: time; freqency; duration; causality.

objective: a statement describing what learners will be able to do as a result of instruction. Formal objectives are meant to have three parts: an activity (what learners will do); conditions (under what circumstances), and standards (how well they will perform).
Example:
Learners will give an oral presentation (activity); speaking for five minutes from prepared notes (conditions); in a manner which is comprehensible to native speakers unused to dealing with non-native speakers (standard).

process syllabus: a syllabus which focuses on the means by which communicative skills will be brought about.

product syllabus: a syllabus which focuses on the outcomes or end products of a language programme.

sequencing: determining the order in which syllabus content will be taught. Content can be sequenced according to difficulty, frequency, or the communicative needs of the learners.

structure: a sequence of grammatical items which form a pattern. The terms structural and grammatical are often used interchangeably to refer to syllabuses in which items are selected and graded largely on grammatical grounds.

synthetic syllabus: a syllabus in which the content is divided into discrete lists of items which are taught separately. The task for the learner is to reintegrate the elements in communication.

syllabus: a specification of what is to be taught in a language programme and the order in which it is to be taught. A syllabus may contain all or any of the following: phonology, grammar, functions, notions, topics, themes, tasks.

task: a unit of planning/teaching containing language data and an activity or sequence of activities to be carried out by the learner on the data.

Further Reading

Anderson, A. and **T. Lynch.** 1988. *Listening.* Oxford: Oxford University Press.
An excellent introduction to the principles and practices of selecting and grading listening tasks.

Brown, G. and **G. Yule.** 1983. *Teaching the Spoken Language.* Cambridge: Cambridge University Press.
This book is a useful complement to the volumes by Anderson and Lynch, and Bygate in this series.

Bygate, M. 1987. *Speaking.* Oxford: Oxford University Press.
Provides a clear introduction to the development of speaking and oral interaction skills along with classroom tasks and activities.

Brumfit, C. J. (ed.). 1984. *General English Syllabus Design.* Oxford: Pergamon.
Provides a range of views on the nature of syllabus design by some of the leading figures in the field.

Clark, J. L. 1987. *Curriculum Renewal in School Foreign Language Learning.* Oxford: Oxford University Press.
Chapters 6 and 7 give a detailed account of two major syllabus planning projects and show how theoretical principles are reflected in syllabus guidelines.

Richards, J. and **T. Rodgers.** 1986. *Approaches and Methods in Language Teaching.* Cambridge: Cambridge University Press.
This book describes the implications for syllabus planning of the different approaches and methods currently in use.

Widdowson, H. G. 1983. *Learning Purpose and Language Use.* Oxford: Oxford University Press.
This book gives a detailed analysis of the issues behind the specific versus general proficiency debate, and sets out the implications of the debate for syllabus design and methodology.

Bibliography

Abbs, B., C. Candlin, C. Edelhoff, T. Moston, and M. Sexton. 1979. *Challenges: Student's Book*. Harlow: Longman.

Allen, J. P. B. 1984. 'General purpose language teaching: a variable focus approach' in C. J. Brumfit (ed.) 1984a.

Anderson, A. and T. Lynch. 1988. *Listening*. Oxford: Oxford University Press.

Bailey, K., C. Madden, and S. Krashen. 1974. 'Is there a "natural sequence" in adult second language learning?' *Language Learning* 24.

Bell, R. 1983. *An Introduction to Applied Linguistics*. London: Batsford.

Breen, M. 1984. 'Process syllabuses for the language classroom' in C. J. Brumfit (ed.) 1984a.

Breen, M. 1985. 'The social context for language learning – a neglected situation?' *Studies in Second Language Acquisition* 7.

Breen, M. 1987. 'Learner contributions to task design' in C. Candlin and D. Murphy (eds.) 1987.

Breen, M. and C. Candlin. 1980. 'The essentials of a communicative curriculum in language teaching.' *Applied Linguistics* 1/2.

Brindley, G. 1984. *Needs Analysis and Objective Setting in the Adult Migrant Education Program*. Sydney: NSW Adult Migrant Education Service.

Brown, G. and G. Yule. 1983. *Teaching the Spoken Language*. Cambridge: Cambridge University Press.

Brumfit, C. J. (ed.) 1984a. *General English Syllabus Design*. Oxford: Pergamon.

Brumfit, C. J. 1984b. *Communicative Methodology in Language Teaching: The Roles of Fluency and Accuracy*. Cambridge: Cambridge University Press.

Bygate, M. 1987. *Speaking*. Oxford: Oxford University Press.

Callaway, D. 1985. *Washington State Adult Refugee ESL Master Plan (Revised)*. Seattle, Wa.: Department of Public Instruction/Department of Social and Health Services.

Candlin, C. 1984. 'Syllabus design as a critical process' in C. J. Brumfit (ed.) 1984a.

Candlin, C. 1987. 'Towards task-based language learning' in C. Candlin and D. Murphy (eds.) 1987.

Candlin, C. and C. Edelhoff. 1982. *Challenges: Teacher's Guide*. London: Longman.

Candlin, C. and **D. Murphy** (eds.) 1987. *Language Learning Tasks.* Englewood Cliffs, NJ: Prentice-Hall.

Chastain, K. 1976. *Developing Second-language Skills.* Chicago: Rand-McNally.

Clark, J. L. 1987. *Curriculum Renewal in School Foreign Language Learning.* Oxford: Oxford University Press.

Clark, J. L. and **J. Hamilton.** 1984. *Syllabus Guidelines 1: Communication.* London: CILT.

Cook, G. (forthcoming) *Discourse.* Oxford: Oxford University Press.

Dick, W. and **L. Carey** 1978. *The Systematic Design of Instruction.* Glenview: Scott Foresman.

Doyle, W. 1979. 'Classroom tasks and students' abilities' in P. Peterson and H. J. Walberg (eds.): *Research on Teaching.* Berkeley, Ca.: McCutchen.

Doyle, W. 1983. 'Academic work.' *Review of Educational Research 53.*

Dubin, F. and **E. Olshtain.** 1986. *Course Design.* Cambridge: Cambridge University Press.

Dulay, H. and **M. Burt.** 1973. 'Should we teach children syntax?' *Language Learning 22.*

Finocchiaro, M. and **C. J. Brumfit.** 1983. *The Functional–Notional Approach: From Theory to Practice.* Oxford: Oxford University Press.

Gronlund, N. 1981. *Measurement and Evaluation in Education.* New York: Macmillan.

Hawaii English Program. 1975. *Hawaii English Program, Report No. 2.* Honolulu: Hawaii Curriculum Center.

Hobbs, J. 1986. *English for Oman.* London: Longman.

Howe, D. 1985. *English Today!* Oxford: Oxford University Press.

Hutchinson, T. and **A. Waters.** 1983. 'Creativity in ESP materials or "Hello! I'm a blood cell" ' in A. Waters (ed.): *Issues in ESP. Lancaster Practical Papers in English Language Education* Vol. 5. Oxford: Pergamon.

Hyltenstam, K. and **M. Pienemann** (eds.) 1985. *Modelling and Assessing Second Language Acquisition.* Clevedon: Multilingual Matters.

Ingram, D. 1984. *Australian Second Language Proficiency Ratings.* Canberra: Department of Immigration and Ethnic Affairs.

Johnston, M. 1985. *Syntactic and Morphological Progressions in Learner English.* Canberra: Department of Immigration and Ethnic Affairs.

Jones, M. and **R. Moar.** 1985. *Listen to Australia.* Sydney: NSW Adult Migrant Education Service.

Krashen, S. 1981. *Second Language Acquisition and Second Language Learning.* Oxford: Pergamon.

Krashen, S. 1982. *Principles and Practice in Second Language Acquisition.* Oxford: Pergamon.

Krashen, S. and **T. Terrell.** 1983. *The Natural Approach.* Oxford: Pergamon.

Lawton, D. 1973. *Social Change, Educational Theory and Curriculum Planning.* London: Hodder and Stoughton.

Long, M. H. 1985. 'A role for instruction in second language acquisition' in K. Hyltenstam and M. Pienemann (eds.) 1985.

Long, M. H. 1987. 'Second language acquisition and the language curriculum.' An interview with D. Nunan. *Prospect* 2/3.

Long, M. H. and **G. Crookes.** 1986. 'Intervention points in second language classroom processes.' *Working Papers* 5/2. Department of English as a Second Language, University of Hawaii.

Macdonald-Ross, M. 1975. 'Behavioural objectives: a critical review' in M. Golby (ed.): *Curriculum Design*. London: Croom Helm.

McDonough, S. 1981. *Psychology in Foreign Language Teaching*. London: Allen and Unwin.

Mager, R. 1975. *Preparing Instructional Objectives*. Palo Alto: Fearon Publishers.

Mager, R. and **C. Clark.** 1963. 'Explorations in student-controlled instruction.' *Psychological Reports* 13.

Mohan, B. 1986. *Language and Content*. Reading, Mass.: Addison-Wesley.

Munby, J. 1978. *Communicative Syllabus Design*. Cambridge: Cambridge University Press.

Nunan, D. 1984. 'Content familiarity and the perception of textual relationships in secondary texts.' *RELC Journal* 15/1.

Nunan, D. 1985. *Language Teaching Course Design: Trends and Issues*. Adelaide: National Curriculum Resource Centre.

Nunan, D. 1987. *The Teacher as Curriculum Developer*. Adelaide: National Curriculum Resource Centre.

Nunan, D. and **J. Burton.** 1985. *Using Learner Data in Designing Language Courses: Workshop Guide*. Adelaide: National Curriculum Resource Centre.

Nunan, D. and **G. Brindley.** 1986. 'A Practical Framework for Learner-Centred Curriculum Development.' Paper presented at the Twentieth Annual TESOL Convention, California.

Nunan, D., M. Tyacke, and **D. Walton.** 1987. *Philosophy and Guidelines for the Omani School English Language Curriculum*. Muscat: Ministry of Education and Youth.

Pearson, I. 1978. *English in Focus: Biological Science*. Oxford: Oxford University Press.

Perry, W. 1987. Review of Bernard A. Mohan 'Language and content.' *TESOL Quarterly* 21/1.

Pienemann, M. 1985. 'Learnability and syllabus construction' in K. Hyltenstam and M. Pienemann (eds.) 1985.

Pienemann, M. and **M. Johnston.** 1987. 'Factors influencing the development of second language proficiency' in D. Nunan (ed.): *Applying Second Language Acquisition*. Adelaide: National Curriculum Resource Centre.

Prabhu, N. S. 1987. *Second Language Pedagogy: A Perspective*. Oxford: Oxford University Press.

Raths, J. 1971. 'Teaching without specific objectives.' *Educational Leadership* April 1971.

Richards, J. 1984. 'Language curriculum development.' *RELC Journal* 15/1.

Richards, J., T. Platt, and **H. Weber.** 1985. *A Dictionary of Applied Linguistics*. London: Longman.

Richards, J. and **T. Rodgers.** 1986. *Approaches and Methods in Language Teaching*. Cambridge: Cambridge University Press.

Rivers, W. 1968. *Teaching Foreign-Language Skills*. Chicago: Chicago University Press.

Rossner, R., P. Shaw, J. Shepherd, J. Taylor, and **P. Davies.** 1979. *Contemporary English, Pupil's Book 1*. London: Macmillan.

Rowntree, D. 1981. *Developing Courses for Studies*. London: McGraw Hill (UK).

Rutherford, W. 1987. *Second Language Grammar: Learning and Teaching*. London: Longman.

Shavelson, R. and **P. Stern.** 1981. 'Research on teachers' pedagogical thoughts, judgements and behaviour.' *Review of Educational Research* 51/4.

Somerville-Ryan, R. D. 1987. 'Taking slow learners to task' in C. Candlin and D. Murphy (eds.) 1987.

Stenhouse, L. 1975. *An Introduction to Curriculum Research and Development*. London: Heinemann.

Stern, H. H. 1984. 'Introduction, review and discussion' in C. J. Brumfit (ed.) 1984a.

Swan, M. and **C. Walter.** 1984. *The Cambridge English Course, Book 1*. Cambridge: Cambridge University Press.

Tyler, R. 1949. *Basic Principles of Curriculum and Instruction*. New York: Harcourt Brace.

Valette, R. and **R. Disick.** 1972. *Modern Language Performance Objectives and Individualisation*. New York: Harcourt Brace.

van Ek, J. 1975. *Threshold Level English*. Oxford: Pergamon.

Whitney, N. 1983. *Checkpoint English*. Oxford: Oxford University Press.

Widdowson, H. G. 1978. *Teaching Language as Communication*. Oxford: Oxford University Press.

Widdowson, H. G. 1979. *Explorations in Applied Linguistics*. Oxford: Oxford University Press.

Widdowson, H. G. 1983. *Learning Purpose and Language Use*. Oxford: Oxford University Press.

Widdowson, H. G. 1984. 'Educational and pedagogic factors in syllabus design' in C. J. Brumfit (ed.) 1984a.

Widdowson, H. G. 1987. 'Aspects of syllabus design' in M. Tickoo (ed.): *Syllabus Design: The State of the Art*. Singapore: Regional English Language Centre.

Wilkins, D. 1976. *Notional Syllabuses*. London: Oxford University Press.

Willing, K. 1988. *Learning Styles in Adult Migrant Education*. Adelaide: National Curriculum Resource Centre.

Wright, T. 1987. *Roles of Teachers and Learners.* Oxford: Oxford University Press.

Wylie, E. and **J. Sunderland.** 1982. *A Course Outline: A Resource for Planning Adult Migrant Courses.* Brisbane: Department of Education.

Yalden, J. 1983. *The Communicative Syllabus: Evolution, Design and Implementation.* Oxford: Pergamon.

Yalden, J. 1984. 'Syllabus design in general education' in C. J. Brumfit (ed.) 1984a.

Index

Entries relate to Sections One, Two, and Three of the text, and to the glossary. References to the glossary are indicated by 'g' after the page number. Titles of publications are given in italics.

Acknowledgements

The publisher would like to thank the following for their permission to reproduce material that falls within their copyright:

Addison-Wesley Publishing Company for an extract from *Language and Content* (1986) by B. Mohan.

Allen & Unwin for an extract from *Psychology in Foreign Language Teaching* (1981) by S. McDonough.

Cambridge University Press for extracts from *Teaching the Spoken Language* (1983) by G. Brown and G. Yule; *Communicative Methodology in Language Teaching: The Roles of Fluency and Accuracy* by C. Brumfit (1984), and *The Cambridge English Course, Book 1* (1984) by M. Swan and C. Walter.

CILT (Centre for Information on Language Teaching) for extracts from *Syllabus Guidelines* (1984) by J. Clark and J. Hamilton.

Commonwealth of Australia Department of Education for an extract from *A Course Outline: A Resource for Planning Adult Migrant Courses* by E. Wylie and J. Sunderland.

Commonwealth of Australia Department of Immigration and Ethnic Affairs for an extract from *Listen to Australia* (1985) by M. Jones and R. Moar.

Commonwealth of Australia National Curriculum Resource Centre for extracts from *Language Teaching Course Design: Trends and Issues* (1985) by D. Nunan, and *Using Learner Data in Designing Language Courses* (1985) by D. Nunan and J. Burton.

Longman Group for extracts from *Challenges: Student's Book* (1979) by B. Abbs, C. Candlin, C. Edelhoff, T. Moston, and M. Sexton, and *Second Language Grammar* (1987) by W. Rutherford.

Macmillan (London and Basingstoke) for an extract from *Contemporary English, Pupil's Book 1* by R. Rossner, P. Shaw, J. Shepherd, J. Taylor, and P. Davies.

Simon and Schuster for an extract from *Issues in ESP. Lancaster Practical Papers in English Language Education, Vol. 5* by T. Hutchinson and A. Waters.

State of Hawaii Department of Education for an extract from *Hawaii English Program, Report No. 2* (1975).

Washington State Office of the Superintendent of Public Instruction for an extract from the *Washington State Adult Refugee ESL Master Plan (Revised)* by D. R. Callaway.

The publisher would also like to thank the following Oxford University Press authors for agreeing to the reproduction of extracts from their books:

D. Howe for an extract from *English Today!* (1985).

I. Pearson for an extract from *English in Focus: Biological Science* (1978).

N. S. Prabhu for an extract from *Second Language Pedagogy* (1987).